P9-CRA-475

The Market

KEY CONCEPTS

Published

The Market

WAGGONER LIBRARY
DISCARD

Alan Aldridge

WAGGONER LIBRARY
TREVECCA NAZARENE UNIVERSITY

polity

Copyright © Alan Aldridge 2005

The right of Alan Aldridge to be identified as Author of this Work has been asserted in accordance with the UK Copyright, Designs and Patents Act 1988.

First published in 2005 by Polity Press

Polity Press
65 Bridge Street
Cambridge CB2 1UR, UK.

Polity Press
350 Main Street
Malden, MA 02148, USA

All rights reserved. Except for the quotation of short passages for the purpose of criticism and review, no part of this publication may be reproduced, stored in a retrieval system, or transmitted, in any form or by any means, electronic, mechanical, photocopying, recording or otherwise, without the prior permission of the publisher.

ISBN: 0-7456-3222-X
ISBN: 0-7456-3223-8 (pb)

A catalogue record for this book is available from the British Library.

Typeset in 10.5 on 12 pt Sabon
by Servis Filmsetting Ltd, Manchester
Printed and bound in Great Britain by TJ International Ltd, Padstow, Cornwall

The publisher has used its best endeavours to ensure that the URLs for external websites referred to in this book are correct and active at the time of going to press. However, the publisher has no responsibility for the websites and can make no guarantee that a site will remain live or that the content is or will remain appropriate.

Every effort has been made to trace all copyright holders, but if any have been inadvertently overlooked the publishers will be pleased to include any necessary credits in any subsequent reprint or edition.

For further information on Polity, visit our website: www.polity.co.uk

Contents

For Meryl Aldridge

Acknowledgements

Without the support of the commissioning editors, Louise Knight and Ellen McKinlay, this project would not exist at all, let alone have come to fruition. Among my colleagues, I should particularly like to thank three. Christian Karner gave me the benefit of his extensive knowledge of social theory, as well as unfailing enthusiasm. Alison Pilnick was supportive of my aim to draw out the significance of Garfinkel's ethnomethodology; I have profited greatly from her expertise on the subject. Meryl Aldridge offered extensive feedback which succeeded – something not to be taken for granted – in being both encouraging and incisive.

Introduction

Given the variety and scale of conflicting interests between individuals and social groups, how does any society succeed in holding together? How can all the complex interactions between millions of citizens possibly be co-ordinated in such a way that chaos is averted? Surely a strong central authority, equipped with objective scientific knowledge and armed with sophisticated weaponry of social surveillance and control, is needed to enforce social order, preventing what the seventeenth-century philosopher Thomas Hobbes called 'a war of all against all'?

The concept of the market provides a radically different answer to these questions. It proposes, in essence, that social order is produced not by centrally planned and administered systems of command and control, but by unplanned mutual adjustments between the myriad of 'ordinary' actors of whom society is composed. Undoubtedly the most influential articulation of this fundamental insight was given, a century after Hobbes, in Adam Smith's contention that individuals pursuing their own interests are guided, as if by 'an invisible hand', to promote not just their own selfish purposes but also the well-being of their society.

Smith's profound insights into the subtle ways in which market transactions can bring about the desirable but unintended goal of social harmony have frequently been misinterpreted as a triumphant hymn of praise to 'the market' as a universal recipe for all social situations. Careful analysis of markets mutates into ideologically-fuelled celebration of *the* market, the *free* market. One specific purpose of this book is to rescue Adam Smith from his latter-day fundamentalist champions.

To do so, it is necessary to disentangle the intricate bundle of description, analysis and prescription that characterizes discourse about the market. Although it regularly claims to be analytic, most theorizing about the market is not innocent: it carries, implicitly or openly, visions of the good society and recipes for how to achieve it. To ignore these prescriptions is to miss a crucial ingredient in the discourse. Indeed, it is precisely at those moments when analysis is thrust to the fore that we shall do well to probe for the prescriptivism that is its almost invariant accomplice.

In chapter 1, the rise of the market is considered in two senses: the growth and expansion of the sphere of market transactions, and the development of the *idea* of the market. These two senses are bound up with each other, since markets do not simply exist 'out there' waiting to be discovered, but are socially and discursively constructed. A key theme of the chapter is the notion that the rise of commerce was a civilizing process. *Doux commerce* – gentle, peaceable commerce – has been held to encourage the kind of virtues that Max Weber identified as the core of the Protestant ethic, including thrift, hard work, deferred gratification, reliability and honesty. These unexciting and unheroic virtues are the bedrock of bourgeois civility, as the critics Karl Marx and Friedrich Engels were well aware.

The concept of the market has tended to polarize opinion. Its supporters claim that the market creates a free, prosperous and dynamic society in which sovereign consumers enjoy the benefits of a vast array of goods and services to satisfy their demands. Critics argue, in contrast, that market societies are characterized by dehumanization and gross inequality. Choice is no more than the fetishization of commodities, and corporations, not consumers, are sovereign. The market does not produce liberty; instead, it sets in train a process of marketization, in which all of social life is colonized by market relations.

The claims of the market's advocates are examined in chapter 2, focusing on a set of powerful contemporary ideologies that provide legitimacy to the political project of promoting markets as the universally optimal mode of social organization. A salient feature of these ideologies is their resistance to any contrary evidence, and their tendency to discount the possibility of market failure.

In chapter 3, markets are examined as complex socio-cultural configurations. Contrary to what is typically implied by free marketeers, the processes by which markets produce and reproduce social order are not automatic. An enormous amount of cultural work is devoted to sustaining faith in the market and trust in the people – the *strangers*, as Georg Simmel emphasized – whom we encounter there. Trust is necessary, but so too is vigilance: a person who is naïvely taken in by the false assurances of the confidence trickster may well be faced with the harsh maxim of the market, 'let the buyer beware'. The dangers of a wholly deregulated market are all too obvious. Abandoning consumers to their fate is likely to destroy the very trust that is needed if markets are to function at all.

The impulse for markets to expand was famously remarked upon by Marx and Engels in the Communist Manifesto of 1848. In the twenty-first century, many markets are becoming global in scope. Whether the trend towards globalization is either desirable or inevitable is the subject of the concluding chapter. Some theories are fatalistic; they imply that resistance is possible only at the margins. If so, then as Ulrich Beck argues political action is futile, and theories that appear to be contesting the hegemony of the market prove to be offering no alternative to capitulation. Perhaps, then, the answer lies neither in war against the market nor surrender, but in an accommodation, whether it be market socialism, or the Third Way, or some other form of 'mixed' economy.

The threatened expansion of the market is not only geographical, but cultural. Neoliberal advocates claim that market forces introduce dynamism into social institutions that otherwise become self-serving, complacent and moribund. Critics fear that in colonizing other domains such as education, the principles of market exchange jeopardize the integrity of the individuals and institutions engaged in those domains. What is at stake is acceptance of or resistance to a process of de-differentiation between social fields that were once governed by their own distinctive norms, values and criteria of excellence.

Description, analysis and prescription: in social theorizing about the market, the first of these fades into the background. The infinite variety of markets is ignored in the quest for analytical abstraction and political prescriptions for how the world should be ordered. The very phrase '*the* market' betrays a kind of essentialism. As an essence, the market provokes strong reactions of support and rejection, reactions which are presented as mutually exclusive. Yet this is divorced from our own experience of markets, which can be simultaneously places of affluence or poverty, excitement or boredom, and human vitality or degradation. Pro- and anti-market ideologies set before us monochrome images of the market which offer but a dim reflection of markets as we create and experience them.

1
The Rise of the Market

The market is among the most divisive concepts in the social sciences. Yet why should this be so, when the dictionary definition of market simply reads: 'Gathering of people for purchase and sale of provisions, livestock *etc.*'?

Markets as we usually understand them, marketplaces, are not controversial. Many cities, towns and villages hold regular markets, where traders set up stalls offering clothes, food, plants, bric-a-brac and domestic equipment for sale. There may be problems with stolen goods, pirated software and shoddy equipment – but these are not the stuff of heated political debate. The dodgy market trader is the anthropologists' trickster: an amoral creature who plays clever and sometimes cruel pranks on his naïve victims. He is both folk devil and popular hero, contemptible villain and loveable rogue.

Early in 2004, viewers in the United Kingdom voted *Only Fools and Horses* the best-ever situation comedy on BBC television. It features the entrepreneurial ventures of Del Boy and Rodney Trotter, market stall holders in Peckham, South London, who regularly sell items of questionable quality and dubious provenance, such as telescopic Christmas trees ('even the Archbishop of Canterbury has one in his front room'). One such enterprise was Peckham Spring Water 'from a natural and ancient source', as indeed it was – the river Thames. Nature needs to be careful when it imitates art. At the same time that the British public was voting for this sitcom, the mighty

Coca-Cola Corporation withdrew from sale in the UK its bottled water, Dasani, after it was revealed that its source was the mains supply to its factory in Sidcup, only eight miles from Peckham. The two cases are not strictly comparable, of course. Coca-Cola subjected its tap water to a variety of sophisticated processes, which unfortunately turned relatively harmless bromide into carcinogenic bromate, whereas Del Boy simply filled his bottles from the tap. One outcome was, however, the same: a mark-up over perfectly drinkable tap water of some 3000 per cent.

In an affluent society nobody is forced to buy from market stalls. Some people enjoy going to markets in search of bargains, while others find them deeply unattractive and think there are no bargains to be found. For example, to their enthusiasts, car boot sales are informal venues where value is created out of second-hand items that sellers would otherwise discard as worthless; to their detractors, and above all to local businesses and trading standards authorities, they represent unfair and dangerously unregulated competition, a public nuisance, and an invitation to petty criminals to sell unsafe, counterfeit and stolen goods (Gregson and Crewe 2003). Why not let the law take its course, let the buyer beware, and leave it at that? We are, and surely should be, more exercised by the capacity of giant transnational corporations to dominate the market domestically and globally.

It is not, then, car boot sales, street markets and stall holders but *the* market, the *free* market, that provokes controversy and polarizes opinion. The market in this sense is not simply a set of social arrangements; it is an ideal, or a vision, or an ideology. It embodies a theory of how human beings relate to one another and how social order is achieved: issues at the heart of all the social sciences.

There is a strong case for arguing that the market has become one of the key concepts through which Western societies understand themselves (Carrier 1997). Through the concept of the market, the West positions itself in opposition to various others: to earlier social formations such as 'primitive', ancient and feudal societies, which are thought to be characterized by non-market exchange; to the Third World, which is seen as developing towards the market system; and communism, a social experiment that sought to suppress the market but failed. As well as spreading across the globe, the market appears also to be colonizing Western societies themselves. With the active support of neoliberal governments, social institutions such as schools and hospitals are forced to introduce market mechanisms into their operations, to make them more efficient and responsive to the needs of their customers. Neoliberalism unleashed a cultural revolution in which people were induced to define themselves simultaneously as the two heroes of market society: consumers and entrepreneurs.

The collapse of communism has been a powerful symbol of the triumph of the market. The deindustrialization of the West is also significant; the factory no longer serves as the dominant image of our times. Factories connote the past, viewed either positively as an era of community, solidarity and collective endeavour, or negatively as an era of class oppression, industrial injury and disease, and environmental degradation. Theories that focused on industrial production are now regularly dismissed as outdated. The obvious casualty has been Marxism, which is often criticized for its 'productivist' bias. Capitalism has been displaced as a key concept; instead, we are offered terms more closely linked to the concept of the market (even if they are used in critique of market ideology), terms such as 'liquid modernity' (Bauman 2000), 'risk society' (Beck 1992), 'network society' (Castells 2000) and 'globalization'. There is even a case for saying that talk of the so-called 'market system' is an ideological device for cloaking the grotesque inequalities of capitalism in a fog of illusions about spontaneous co-ordination and the diffusion of power throughout society (Galbraith 2004).

Within the social sciences, the discipline that has taken the market both as object of enquiry and tool of analysis is, obviously, economics. Yet there is a puzzle. Economics texts have astonishingly little to say explicitly about the concept of the market itself (Callon 1998: 1). Instead, they typically discuss aspects of the market, such as market equilibrium and market failure. Perhaps, adapting Flaubert, the market is like the author of a book or God in his universe: present everywhere and visible nowhere. This analogy points to an important conclusion: the market is not simply an object waiting for economists and others to discover and study it. Wholly, or in part, it is through economics and other bodies of discourse that the market is socially constructed. One clear sign of this is that economists are less concerned with describing the characteristics of markets in all their rich empirical detail, than they are with providing abstract analytical models of how the market works, and deriving from this prescriptions of what needs to be done to ensure that markets operate effectively. Notoriously, their recipe is often laissez-faire: leave the market alone so that it can do its good work without interference.

Elements of Market Society

Following Lindblom (2002: 52–8), we can identify eight essential elements of the market system.

Liberty

A market system is characterized by relative freedom under the law to pursue one's own interests – in contrast to slave, feudal, caste or totalitarian societies.

Property

Property involves rights over the control and use of resources, including the right to deny access to other people. As Saunders explains (1995: 3), private ownership of property involves three rights enforceable by law: exclusive control and use of the property; exclusive benefit from the exploitation of the property; and disposal of the property as one sees fit. Property rights extend to one's body; hence the capitalist market is based upon freedom of contract. Property rights are a condition of individual liberty, and foster the entrepreneurial spirit.

Quid Pro Quo

Lindblom stresses that the market is a system of exchanges, where one party to a transaction offers goods or services contingent on the supply of reciprocal benefits, typically in the form of money.

Money

A barter system, in which exchanges take place without the medium of money, is inefficient because it requires that each of the parties to an exchange is able to offer something that the other wants. The defining characteristic of money is that it is widely accepted as payment for goods and services, and to settle debts. Originally, money took the form of material objects that were valued for themselves, such as coins made of precious metals. As money evolved, coins and notes became tokens whose value was the purchasing power stored in them. The evolution of money as an abstract store of value and medium of exchange was closely bound up with the rise of the nation-state.

Activity for Sale

In a market economy, activities are not primarily oriented to the production of goods and services for domestic consumption. Instead, production is geared to supplying goods and services for sale, with payment typically made in money rather than kind.

Intermediaries

As the market expands and the division of labour increases, so the chain of intermediaries necessarily grows longer and more complex. 'Middlemen' may be seen in populist discourse as parasites, but this is a gross misconception, since they are essential to the efficient functioning of the market system.

Entrepreneurs

Entrepreneurs are a special category of intermediary; they bear the risk of introducing new products and new methods of production. They create factories and office buildings, machines, equipment, parts, and other inputs for making hardware. To advocates of the market, entrepreneurs are heroes; in Lindblom's words (2002: 57): 'They are the moving spirits in the market system, the participants who make not only the most frequent but the most consequential decisions.' They assemble the factors of production – the workers, land, factories, offices, machinery, equipment, parts – whose efficient utilization explains the productivity of market systems.

Collectives

Although the free market celebrates individualism, not least in the figure of the entrepreneur, the firm has always been a key agent in market societies. Contemporary capitalism is characterized by large corporations, and this has profound implications for discourse on the market, not least because of the power that corporations wield in it.

The Invisible Hand: Social Co-ordination without a Co-ordinator

How is social order possible? Why does society hold together, instead of flying apart in an endless war of conflicting interests? Why is human life not 'solitary, poor, nasty, brutish, and short'? How is the co-ordination of millions of human beings accomplished? Who are the co-ordinators?

In the history of social thought the most common answer to the problem of social order has been to invoke the idea of an elite corps of rulers who would direct the actions of their social inferiors. Plato's *Republic* is a leading example of this approach to the problem. In Plato's ideal just society, the state is ruled by philosophers; lovers of knowledge whose personal qualities and education qualify them to direct the activities of the other two great groupings of society, the military and the common people. To guarantee their commitment to the community, the rulers are not permitted to own private property and cannot learn who their children are. Social co-ordination can be achieved only by direction, and only the few are fit to govern.

Two thousand years after Plato, the sociologist Auguste Comte envisaged a society ruled by 'positive' philosophers. They would be a body of intellectuals well versed in scientific methods. Politicized sectional conflicts would be replaced by scientific consensus. Standing outside and above class interests, the positive philosophers would speak for and enforce the common good. They would compel social classes to fulfil their reciprocal obligations and to refrain from exploiting one another. The division of labour, which potentially leads to the dissolution of social bonds, would be channelled for the well-being of society. Thus the ideals of progress and social order would be harmonized.

Critics of Comte's vision have emphasized its authoritarianism. Comte was quite clear that social order cannot arise spontaneously from civil society, that is to say from the social interactions of people going about their everyday business. Social order has to be imposed from above. Society, like nature, operates according to laws, and it is foolish to think we can ignore them. Positive philosophers are schooled in the laws of society, and have the duty of ensuring that people comply with them. This implies what would later be called a 'command and control' model of social regulation.

While the details of Plato's, Comte's and other thinkers' models of the good society may be unconvincing or repugnant, surely the basic principles are sound? Social order depends on a judicious balance of coercion and consent. Co-ordination of a whole society needs people to plan the co-ordination and others to carry it out. As in theology so in social science: design implies a designer, divine in one case, human in the other. But does it?

Historically, the least common answer to the problem of social order envisages co-ordination by mutual adjustment – paradoxically, co-ordination without a co-ordinator. Lindblom (2002: 27–30) offers examples of stray thinkers who have taken this position. For example, Polybius observed, in the second century BC, that Roman institutions had not been designed centrally but had evolved through unplanned trial and error. In the eighteenth century, Montesquieu had a similar insight about social laws and customs. In the natural sciences, Isaac Newton's *Principia* of 1687 explained the motion of stars and planets in terms of the forces of attraction and repulsion between them. God set the system in motion, but it operates now without further intervention by God and through its own internal mechanisms. This is the God of the Deists.

Deist philosophers such as Voltaire argued that belief in God could and should be founded on reasoning from evidence. Deists relied heavily on the argument from design: the argument that various features of the world, such as the complex structure and functioning of the human eye, are best explained as products of a divine blueprint. God has created things according to a design, and each creature tends to fulfil the purpose assigned to it by God.

While upholding the existence of God, Deists rejected the idea of faith based on special divine revelations through sacred texts or charismatic leaders. Revelation calls for irrational faith, and promotes superstition, credulity, priestly deceptions and tyranny. Religion based on revelation is ethnocentric; our God, our saints and prophets, our creeds and our commandments are superior to yours. Natural religion, that is religion without special revelations, is based on the universal power of human reason. We observe the world and deduce the existence of God from it.

By the end of the eighteenth century, the key feature of Deism was belief in a God who created the world and ordained its laws, but who now refrains from further intervention in his creation. God is a watchmaker whose watch needs no repair. It follows that there is no point, or at least no pay-off, in offering him sacrifices or prayers. A remote absentee, the God of Deism is in a precarious position. Belief in him loses most of its emotional appeal; if we can explain the order in the world without reference to his purposes, we shall not have lost much. Deism, in short, prepared the ground for atheism, and made the thought of co-ordination without a co-ordinator more palatable.

Our contemporary understanding of social co-ordination by mutual adjustment has been shaped by the work of three great theorists: Sigmund Freud, Charles Darwin and Adam Smith.

Sigmund Freud's work analyses the psyche as an arena of mutual adjustment between conflicting principles. We are not, as we might fondly think, ruled by a sovereign intelligence. Instead, according to classical psychoanalytic theory our psychic apparatus is made up of three interacting components: the *ego*, representing our conscious reason and common sense, and governed by the reality principle; the *superego*, in which our self-observation and self-criticism develops, governing our ethical and moral standards of conduct; and the *id*, the unorganized, instinctual parts of our psyche, governed by the pleasure principle that seeks immediate gratification, and is dark and inaccessible to consciousness. Psychic health is a question not of a central authority imposing discipline, but of balance and adjustment.

Darwin's *Origin of Species* (1859) sees evolution as the adjustment of organisms to their environment. The key principle is natural selection, through which the organisms best suited to their environment are the ones that tend to survive. Survival of the fittest – a phrase coined not by Darwin but by the sociologist, Herbert Spencer – is achieved not so much by killing rivals as by reproductive success. Organisms that happen to have characteristics which are suited to their environment, or which enable them to survive cataclysms, will thrive; they will pass on those characteristics to their offspring, whereas organisms that lack suitable characteristics will struggle, leaving fewer or no descendants.

The chance variations within species selected by nature were not *designed* to fit in with the environment. There is no design, no intention, no goal. Creatures do not develop characteristics in order to survive; they survive because they happen to have those characteristics. Evolution is blind, serves no higher purpose and is not aiming at anything.

Among advocates of the market as a system of unplanned mutual accommodation there is universal agreement that the classic text is *An Enquiry into the Nature and Causes of The Wealth of Nations* (1776) by Adam Smith. It has become a totem of neoliberal thought – a questionable development, since his work is subtler and far less dogmatic than many of his latter-day acolytes allow. Adam Smith deserves to be rescued from his followers.

Seventeenth-century philosophers had sought to answer questions about the innate qualities of humanity. They took this to require investigation, inevitably speculative, of 'the state of nature', that is to say the human condition before government has been instituted. The role of government was to rectify the deficiencies of the state of nature. Clearly, radically opposed political programmes followed from divergent depictions of the state of nature. For Hobbes, the state of nature was a lawless and amoral condition in which individuals were free to do whatever they deemed necessary for survival. It was 'a war . . . of every man against every man', in which life was, in his famously stark assessment, 'solitary, poor, nasty, brutish, and short'. Human beings are therefore rational to surrender their freedoms to a monarch wielding absolute power as the surest guarantee against falling back into the abject condition of the state of nature. For Locke, in contrast, the state of nature is governed by human reason, which teaches us to respect other people and their possessions. Individual liberty requires private property; a task of government is therefore to establish a body of law and the institutions to administer and enforce property rights. Locke suggests that the arbitrary dictates of Hobbes's absolute monarch would be a dubious improvement on the state of nature even as Hobbes conceived it. What is required is a government that promotes the well-being of society, acquiring its legitimacy from the continuing support of the majority of the people.

A century later, Smith argued that humans have an innate propensity 'to truck, barter, and exchange one thing for another (1976/1776: 25). This propensity is a defining characteristic of human nature, and not found in other animals; dogs, he remarked, do not exchange bones with other dogs. Commerce is not demeaning but ennobling. The propensity is innate in humans, but can be expressed fully only in a market society. Running through his work is the implication that governments should interfere as little as possible with market exchanges, and that neither combinations of firms (cartels) nor combinations of workers (unions) should act as restraints on trade or labour. The market accords with human nature and should therefore normally be left alone unless there is good reason to intervene.

Smith's reference to 'the invisible hand' is widely quoted and frequently misunderstood. It is not a religious or mystical idea, but a metaphor designed to capture the remarkable way in which co-ordination is produced by a market system. Although he used the phrase only once in each of his two major works, the idea permeates his thought. In *The Wealth of Nations* (1976/1776: 456) he wrote that although each individual is seeking his own gain the outcome is to maximize national wealth and therefore to further the public interest: 'he intends only his own gain, and he is in this, as in many other cases, led by an invisible hand to promote an end which was no part of his intention'. In his earlier work, *The Theory of Moral Sentiments* (1976/1759: 184–5), Smith argues that an invisible hand leads economic agents, again pursuing their own self-interest, to act in ways which bring about a wide diffusion of wealth throughout the nation.

The point of the metaphor of the invisible hand is to draw attention to the paramount importance of the *unintended* consequences of economic action: individual self-interest produces social co-operation. Here the market operates in a manner that seems contrary to common sense. When we think of co-operation we tend to imagine a situation where everyone is consciously helping everyone else in an activity governed by a strong sense of community. We do not think of co-operation as impersonal and unintended – but that is precisely how markets typically function. Any engagement in market activity is, whether we realize it or not, a vote that sets off a chain reaction of unintended consequences. It is not intention but interdependence that is crucial.

The market system achieves co-ordination 'invisibly' through interactions between sellers and buyers, supply and demand. The specific mechanism for this is, as Smith saw, the price system. Prices have three functions (Friedman 1980: 14–24):

To Transmit Information   The price system not only transmits information but does so efficiently, targeting those who need it. The people sending the information have an interest in ensuring it gets to the right people, while the people who need it have an interest in seeking it out. This is the exact opposite of spam e-mail, which delivers worthless noise indiscriminately to all and sundry.

To Provide Incentives   Prices provide incentives to act on information. Rising prices for their goods encourage producers to increase output, while falling prices have the reverse effect. Hence the public gets more of what it wants and less of what it does not want. The price system also encourages producers to satisfy consumer demand by using resources as efficiently as possible.

To Distribute Income   Although this is the most controversial function of the price mechanism, advocates of the free market insist that it is a corollary of the other two functions. It is self-contradictory to be in favour of the market but opposed to social inequality.

The Wealth of Nations famously begins with an analysis of the manufacture of pins. Ten people working in a pin factory and dividing the tasks between them – Smith tells us there are eighteen different operations – can manufacture over 48,000 pins a day. How many pins could one person working alone produce? Not one tenth of 48,000 but far fewer – perhaps twenty. If we also accept that specialist machinery is itself a product of the division of labour, so that a lone worker would lack such equipment, we might conclude that he would do well to produce even one pin a day. Smith was not idolizing factory life; instead, it was a dramatically simple demonstration of the benefits of the division of labour. What is true of pins is true of all everyday items, whether food, clothes or shelter. The division of labour delivers benefits to rich and poor alike.

Like other thinkers of the Scottish and French Enlightenment, Smith confronted the problem that the modern commercial societies of their times were more affluent but less equal than earlier types of society based respectively on hunting and gathering, pasture and agriculture. Was this progress?

Smith undoubtedly saw affluence and wealth as the same thing. But what of the suggestion, put forward by the anthropologist Marshall Sahlins (1972: 1–39), that if an affluent society is one in which all the people's material wants are easily satisfied, then there are two routes to affluence: the path of economic growth, and the 'Zen' way of renouncing desire? The former is the path of industrial societies. Wants are potentially infinite, which implies that the means to achieve them are necessarily scarce. 'Modern capitalist societies', Sahlins argues (1972: 3), 'however richly endowed, dedicate themselves to the proposition of scarcity. Inadequacy of economic means is the first principle of the world's wealthiest peoples' – a principle enshrined in economic theory.

The second way to affluence, the path of renunciation, characterizes hunter-gatherer societies. Viewed from a Western economist's perspective, the world of hunter-gatherers appears a life of poverty, an incessant, exhausting quest for subsistence, leaving little time for any form of leisure or creative endeavour. And yet, Sahlins says, although they have few possessions they are not 'poor'. Poverty is a social status, a relation between people. Nor are resources 'scarce' in hunting-and-gathering societies; typically, they are plentiful. On this account, poverty and scarcity are creations of industrial civilization.

Smith had an optimistic belief in progress; he held that modern commercial societies bring not only economic growth but also a wide diffusion of prosperity. Such societies may be vastly unequal, but even so the masses are far better off materially (and morally) than in non-market societies. General prosperity outweighs social inequality. Nor is it simply a question of prosperity; Smith joined with other Enlightenment thinkers, including Montesquieu, Condorcet, Hegel and Thomas Paine, in extolling the civilizing virtues of *doux commerce* – gentle, peaceable commerce. The calm pursuit of self-interest through market exchanges fosters the bourgeois values of industriousness, punctuality, reliability and trustworthiness. Such virtues may be despised as unworthy and unheroic – they do not befit the haughty aristocrat and the proud warrior – or they may be prized as the bedrock of a civilized life. To some degree, Smith argued, commercial society makes merchants of us all; which is far from saying, as some latter-day followers do, that we have become self-interested 'economic men'. Merchants are concerned for their good reputation; lose that, and their business goes under. For the same reason, modern corporations strive to cultivate their brand image. All this is in contrast to societies geared to war and conquest, piracy and looting. So it is, as Hirschman argues (1977), that the orderly pursuit of self-interest was thought to conquer the unruly passions.

Smith's work made a major contribution to shaping one dimension of what Charles Taylor calls 'the social imaginary' (Taylor 2004). This concept refers to the ways in which ordinary people imagine and make sense of their society, ways which are expressed more through symbols, rituals and legends than in formal philosophical systems or scientific theories. The social imaginary is an inextricable mix of fact and value, creating meaning and conferring legitimacy; it is not the property of intellectuals, though it may originate with them. Taylor argues that 'the economy' is one of the three dominant elements in the social imaginary of Western civilization; the other two are the public sphere and the democratically self-governing people. Not only that: the economy has tended to be seen as the most important element of the three, so that the goal of society is taken to be economic success and prosperity.

For Smith, history was not an endless cycle of the rise and fall of civilizations; instead, he saw free market commercial societies as the culmination of a series of stages of social development. In arguing in this fashion, Smith showed himself to be thoroughly liberal in spirit, since meliorism – the doctrine that social and political institutions can be improved through human efforts – is a core feature of liberal thought (Gray 1986).

Freedom, Liberalism and the Market

The political philosophers of Ancient Greece and Rome focused on the question, what is the ideal form of government? Is it a monarchy, a republic, a democracy? On what criteria should the rulers be selected: birth, wealth or merit? Underlying these questions was the assumption that freedom entailed participation in the affairs of state.

In the modern world, a second set of questions is no less important: how much government shall there be? What are the boundaries between public life, the legitimate province of political authority, and a private sphere into which government should not, except in crises, intrude?

Arguably the most influential answer to these questions is to be found in liberalism. At its core are the principles of liberty, rights and individualism. As Slater and Tonkiss (2001: 29) put it: 'Liberalism takes individual liberty as a normative foundation of social life and looks for mechanisms – like the market and representative democracy – that will ensure order while not compromising freedoms.' Liberalism assumes that freedom requires that the private sphere is protected from the encroachments of the state. In the contemporary world, liberalism has recognized another great system of political thought and practice as its deadliest enemy: socialism.

The debate between liberalism and socialism was addressed in three powerful books written during the Second World War: Joseph Schumpeter's *Capitalism, Socialism, and Democracy*, Karl Polanyi's *The Great Transformation* and Friedrich Hayek's *The Road to Serfdom*. Nazism was facing defeat by a coalition of capitalism and Soviet-style socialism; yet both capitalism and socialism had sought an accommodation with the Nazi regime. What, then, was the relationship between these three ideologies and the socio-political orders on which they rested? What prospect did the future hold?

Schumpeter and Polanyi concluded, despite their radically opposed political commitments, that liberal civilization was in its death throes. The heyday of the liberal order had been the years of relative peace in Europe, from the Congress of Vienna in 1815, which established a supposed balance of power between nation-states after the defeat of Napoleon at Waterloo, to the outbreak of the First World War. In retrospect, 1914 was commonly identified as a watershed that marked the passing of the old order. Subsequent events appeared to confirm this: the fall of Schumpeter's beloved Austro-Hungarian empire; the Russian Revolution of 1917; Stalin's purges, and his ruthless programme of industrialization and collectivization implemented in the Five-Year Plans; the Wall Street Crash of 1929; the Great Depression; the collapse of the international monetary system based on the Gold Standard; Franklin D. Roosevelt's New Deal; the failure of the League of Nations; and the ascent of Fascism and Nazism. When it became clear that the Allies would win the Second World War, people talked of the coming Age of Reconstruction; but what kind of social, political and economic order would be created out of the rubble of liberal civilization?

Schumpeter argued that the future lay, unfortunately in his view as a conservative-minded liberal, with some form of socialist collectivism. The liberal order had undermined itself, but this was not, as Marx had believed, due to an unmanageable economic crisis caused by the falling rate of profit. Nor was it caused, as some economists argued, by the growth of giant oligopolistic corporations. On the contrary, oligopolies and monopolies were prominent in creating new goods, services, technologies and modes of delivery; they were not incompatible with the entrepreneurial spirit, but had the capacity to engage in the 'creative destruction' of old forms that is the hallmark of enterprise.

Despite the economic hardships of the 1930s, the root causes of the decline, on Schumpeter's account, were social and cultural. Capitalism had been able to regulate itself only by implementing 'anti-capitalist' policies, which included an expanded role for the state and the public sector generally, redistributive measures to reduce social inequality, concessions to labour unions, anti-trust legislation, price controls, and high levels of public expenditure on welfare and social security. The bourgeoisie and the strata of society that supported it were in decline and under threat. For Marx, capitalism would create its own gravediggers in the form of the proletariat; for Schumpeter, this role was being performed by radical intellectuals who mobilized the discontent of the masses, using the media to spread their gospel of revolutionary struggle. Ideologues and agitators were free to exploit the short-run crises of capitalism. Ironically, in the long run the benefits of capitalism would have become evident; but the long run would never be given a chance to materialize. Capitalism was undeservedly doomed; socialism would take its place, and *might* (but probably would not) succeed.

Schumpeter was fearful of the socialist future. One reading of his work is that it was not so much a prediction as a warning (Muller 2003: 297): unless liberalism's supporters can find ways to address the cultural contradictions of capitalism, socialism will be the inevitable outcome.

Like Schumpeter, Polanyi saw the causes of the decline of the old order as endemic; unlike Schumpeter, he welcomed the socialist future. *The Great Transformation* begins dramatically: 'Nineteenth century civilization has collapsed' (Polanyi 1957/1944: 3). The liberal order rested on four pillars, all of which had crumbled: the balance of power, the international gold standard, the self-regulating market and the liberal state. Of these, the self-regulating market was fundamental both to the liberal order and to its self-annihilation.

The market, according to Polanyi, brought costs that society ultimately could not bear. The market 'disembedded' the economy from society, turning labour, land and money into commodities. The outcome was widespread unemployment, poverty in cities and destitution in the countryside, depredation of the environment and destruction of community and kinship networks. Fascism, Nazism, Soviet Communism and the New Deal were all responses to the crisis, with the common aim of 're-embedding' the economy in society. Polanyi believed that the market could be regulated and controlled while retaining the democratic virtues of the liberal way: 'Socialism is, essentially, the tendency inherent in an industrial civilization to transcend the self-regulating market by consciously subordinating it to a democratic society' (Polanyi 1957/1944: 234).

Faced with the claim that liberalism has had its day, Hayek's *The Road to Serfdom* strikes a defiant note. The whole book aims to be an exposé of what Hayek takes to be socialism's false promises and hypocrisy – the book is wryly dedicated 'to the socialists of all parties'. Far from being the natural successor to liberalism, socialism is an atavistic throwback that actually paved the way for Nazism. Socialism does not liberate us from barbarism but delivers us over to it. Arguing that the West has gradually abandoned, even forgotten, the liberal principles on which civilization is founded, Hayek celebrates the achievements of liberalism and capitalism, ending with this declaration: 'The guiding principle that a policy of freedom for the individual is the only truly progressive policy remains as true today as it was in the nineteenth century' (Hayek 1994/1944: 262).

Hayek's classic liberalism stands in direct line of descent from Adam Smith. He saw that the rise of commercial society brought with it a dawning recognition of the power of co-ordination by mutual adjustment. We should cultivate these spontaneous forces of society as much as we can, considering coercion as a weapon of last resort. Significantly, Hayek disliked the term laissez-faire, which he saw as an expression of a rigid dogma. 'The liberal argument', he tells us, 'is in favor of making the best possible use of the forces of competition as a means of co-ordinating human efforts, not an argument for leaving things just as they are' (1994/1944: 41). Like Smith before him, Hayek insists that a vital role of the state is to develop a strong legal system as an essential framework for social order, not least for promoting and protecting competition.

Hayek's practical engagement with the ways in which markets actually operate is congruent with Adam Smith's approach, and characterizes the 'Austrian' school of economics, of which he became the best-known representative. For this school, as for Smith, market economies are dynamic systems in which entrepreneurs strive to design new goods and services and new modes of delivering them.

Two further aspects of the Austrian approach deserve emphasis (Gamble 1996: 66–74). First, whereas orthodox neo-classical economic models operate on the simplifying assumption that actors in a market have perfect knowledge, the Austrian school rejects this, insisting that knowledge is always imperfect and widely dispersed in human societies. Second, the Austrian school holds that economic costs and benefits are irreducibly subjective. A key concept is 'opportunity cost': by choosing any one course of action, we necessarily forego the benefits of alternatives. Assessments of opportunity costs are subjective. The economic system is powered by knowledge that is subjective, widely distributed, and inaccessible to any central authority. Here Hayek and his colleagues were making a point that lay at the heart of Smith's analysis of the market. Immediately following his metaphor of the invisible hand, Smith asserts that no legislator or politician can be better placed than we are to judge the particularities of our own 'local situation' (1976/1776: 456).

On this line of reasoning, the socialist dream of collectivizing knowledge is therefore founded on an illusion, and ruinous for liberty. We should resist the plausible appeal of leaving planning to the worthy intentions of experts because, Hayek warns (1994/1944: 62), 'From the saintly and single-minded idealist to the fanatic is often but a step.' Or as Smith put it, the last person to whom such power should be entrusted is 'a man who had folly and presumption enough to fancy himself fit to exercise it' (Smith 1976/1776: 456).

For all his emphasis on studying markets as they actually operate, Hayek decisively rejects as misguided any search for a middle way between competition and central planning. He is not arguing for a mixed economy with a significant public sector. Planning and competition are antithetical; or rather, the only economic role for planning is planning for competition.

Hayek shared a concern that will recur throughout this book: the specious separation of 'the economy' from the rest of society, as though there were a category of asocial 'economic' actions that could be analysed without reference to human culture. He disliked the very term 'economy', which he saw as fatally misleading. The word derives from the Greek words *oikos*, a house, and *nomos*, law; hence the root meaning of *oikonomia* is management of a household. To Hayek this implied a delimited domain that could be rationally planned, monitored and controlled – precisely as the economy could not be! An unforeseen consequence of the ascendancy of the economy within the modern social imaginary was a growing conviction that economists were a species of social engineer who could intervene to make dramatic improvements in the way the system worked. Alarmed at this prospect, Hayek tried to introduce the term *catallaxy*, similarly derived from the Greek and meaning a spontaneous system of voluntary exchanges – in other words, the market.

If, in the market, we pursue our interests, these include not just our material wants but our emotional commitments and our highest ideals. And if there is no such thing as 'the economy', there is no 'economic' planning; what is called economic planning is in fact planning for the whole of life (Muller 2003: 367) – which is why it is so lethal to liberty.

One theme that recurs in Hayek's work is the seductive nature of socialism. It is incontestable, he argues, that 'the promise of greater freedom has become one of the most effective weapons of socialist propaganda and that the belief that socialism would bring freedom is genuine and sincere' (Hayek 1994/1944: 31). Not only is this an illusion; in the hands of the Soviet authorities, as of all authorities, it is a deliberate sham. He comments acidly on 'the complete perversion of language, the change of meaning of the words by which the ideals of the new regimes are expressed. The worst sufferer in this respect is, of course, the word "liberty" ' (Hayek 1994/ 1944: 173). It is worth noting that George Orwell published a favourable review of *The Road to Serfdom* four years before the appearance of his own *1984*.

Hayek's celebration of the liberal social order rests on a robust assertion of individual human rights. Even if his critique of socialism is taken, does contemporary capitalism live up to the liberal ideal? Is the capitalist market an arena of freely chosen exchanges between entrepreneurs and consumers?

What about the massive concentrations of power in giant transnational corporations?

Like many other liberals, as Gamble comments, Hayek finds it difficult to come to terms with the economic and social might of corporations, even though it calls into question his analysis of knowledge as widely distributed among individual actors. His belief in co-ordination by mutual adjustment – Smith's invisible hand – makes him draw back from advocating robust anti-trust policies designed to smash concentrations of power. Instead, he is inclined to the view that corporations will be reined in by competition; if so, concentrations of power can be viewed as normal and legitimate outcomes of the operation of free markets.

Perhaps the greatest irony in Hayek's position is the conflict between his attempts to defend corporations against political trust-busting interventions, and his opposition to all forms of bureaucracy as sapping individual initiative and self-reliance. Hayek is obviously deeply troubled by the growth of bureaucratic corporations and by the tendency in modern society for most people to become employees, and therefore dependent on others for their livelihood. A free market and a limited role for the state are the aspirations of entrepreneurs, not of employees. Sheltered from the bracing winds of market forces, bureaucratic workers have a dangerous affinity with socialism.

Christian, Civic Republican and Marxian Responses

Moral opposition to the principles, values and ethos of market society has a long pedigree that stretches back beyond the age of industrialization to the early modern era, the Middle Ages and classical Greece. Following Muller (2003), we can distinguish two broad strands in the pre-industrial critique of market society: the Christian tradition and civic republicanism.

The Christian tradition drew many of its core ideas from the Greeks. They did not spurn affluence, which they saw as necessary for active participation in the life of the city-state. To them the danger was that the *pursuit* of wealth can become insatiable, destroying the balance that is essential to the good life and the harmony of the virtues. In classical Greek thought, commerce was tolerated but not admired. Merchants, Aristotle reasoned, should be denied an active part in the political life of the ideal society.

The Christian Church took this suspicion of commerce and turned it into outright condemnation. There were many sources in the New Testament, including sayings of Jesus ('It is easier for a camel to go through the eye of a needle, than for a rich man to enter into the kingdom of God'; 'Sell that thou hast and give to the poor and thou shalt have treasure in heaven'; 'Lay not up for yourselves treasures upon earth, where moth and rust doth corrupt') and preaching by St Paul ('the love of money is the root of all evil'), that lent support to the Church's judgement that avarice was one of the seven deadly sins. Avarice was fifth in order of importance; the others were pride, envy, anger, sloth, gluttony and lechery. They were called deadly because they would destroy the capacity for love (the supreme virtue) if they took hold of a person's soul (Hamilton, B. 1986: 132–41). What else was the pursuit of profit but avarice, the warped love of money?

Since it was assumed one person's profit was bound to be another person's loss, commerce was condemned on grounds of inequity; but as commerce started to flourish in the late medieval period, so Christian opinion became more nuanced. Instead of blanket disapproval, a distinction was drawn between legitimate and illegitimate commercial activities. Labour, private property and trade were useful; the paradigm case to be stigmatized was usury, lending money at interest. The Hebrew scriptures forbade the people from lending money at interest to their 'brother', but allowed it when 'strangers' were the debtors; this meant that Jews could lend at interest only to non-Jews. Medieval Christian theologians interpreted the scriptures differently: since all people are my brother and no one is a stranger, usury is always sinful. Money, the Church taught, was sterile, so making money from money was parasitic. The Catholic Church's prohibition of usury was long-standing, and persisted well into the eighteenth century; the Protestant Churches were only marginally less hostile. What was an abomination to Christians was judged fitting for Jews, who were held to be damned anyway because of their refusal to receive Christ.

Muller emphasizes the link between ideologies of the market and anti-semitism. Money was disgusting, filthy lucre; Jews were depicted as foul-smelling; both were unclean and polluting. Specifically, 'the Jew' became an icon of avarice. Forced out of land-owning, farming and the crafts, Jews increasingly turned to forms of commercial activity that were simultaneously necessary to Christian society and vilified by it. The complex hypocrisy this entailed was brilliantly captured, of course, in Shakespeare's *The Merchant of Venice*.

If Christian hostility to market society was based on accusations of sin and avarice, civic republicanism focused on corruption and self-interest, both of which encouraged dereliction of public duty in pursuit of private gain. The civic republican approach can be traced back to classical roots, specifically to the Aristotelian opinion that the good life consists in active participation in the life of the political community. 'In general', Muller comments (2003: 13–14), 'the civic tradition identified "virtue" with devotion to the public good and "liberty" with participation in political life'. A life free from toil, which in ancient Greece required ownership of land and slaves, was a prerequisite of full participation in public life. Commercial activity was not sinful, but diversionary.

Against this historical backdrop, the arguments of Adam Smith and others in the tradition of what Muller calls 'civil jurisprudence' offered not just a more favourable but a more objective and penetrating analysis of the values and modus operandi of market society. Rather than selectively condemning aspects of the market, they sought to understand it. Social order exists for the benefit of us all. In place of Christian preoccupation with the world to come, thinkers such as Smith and Hobbes concentrated on this life and the happiness it could offer. And instead of the civic republican quest for honour and glory and the Christian cultivation of faith and piety, they preached the virtues of *doux commerce*.

Their favourable analysis of commerce implies, as Taylor points out (2004: 74), an affirmation of the value of ordinary life and the common people. Its thrust is anti-elitist. It dethrones what had been seen as 'higher' forms of life: the heroism of warrior society, the contemplative life prized by the Ancient Greeks, and the other-worldly ascetic orientation of

Christian monasticism. It ushered in the modern emphasis on the economy, family life and personal relationships.

Their philosophy could be profoundly unsettling, not least because of its this-worldly orientation and therefore potentially secularizing implications. Their analysis of society no longer grounds it in a divinely ordained sacred cosmos. The modern world is defined by religious faith, not by religious culture (Sommerville 1992). In the Middle Ages, religion provided the categories of thought through which the world was understood, so that atheism and agnosticism were not so much forbidden as unthinkable. With the Enlightenment, this all-embracing religious culture gradually dissolved, and religion was reconfigured as individual faith: reasoned and self-aware affirmations of personal belief and commitment.

One particularly troubling aspect of Smith's thought was his uncoupling of intentions and consequences. Christian moralists and civic republicans put good intentions at the centre of their prescriptions. Smith's emphasis on unintended consequences can be read as a disturbing refutation of the value of preaching and propaganda (Muller 2003: 64).

The civil jurisprudence tradition can be traced back to Roman civil law, which recognized commerce as a vital ingredient of the Roman Empire. Private property and the rule of law were essential to protect citizens from unjustified actions of the state. This concern for citizens and their possessions reveals the individualism that was latent in the tradition until later thinkers unlocked it.

If Adam Smith stands as the greatest, most original and subtle advocate of the market system, Karl Marx and Friedrich Engels must surely be its most penetrating opponents. Their analysis drew on both Christian and civic republican critiques of the market, while radically secularizing and modernizing them. They confronted Smith directly, turning his arguments upside down in characteristically Marxian fashion.

To Marx and Engels, Smith's picture of *doux commerce* as a civilizing process was utterly preposterous; they even shared private jokes about it. When Engels finally severed his links with his family's textile firm in order to devote himself to the cause of revolutionary socialism, he wrote to Marx: 'Hurrah! Today marks the end of the *doux commerce*, and

I am a free man' (quoted in Hirschman 1977: 62n). To them, commerce was not peace but war – class and imperialistic war. Marx ridiculed the idea of *doux commerce* in *Das Kapital*, stressing the violence that was bound up with international trade. It may not have been as elevated as the hero's quest for glory, but the entrepreneur's lust for profit was no less ruthless.

Marx and Engels refashioned Christian hostility towards usury into diatribes against speculation, and a critique of the exploitative relationship between capitalists and proletarians. Their labour theory of value, taken from the classical economist David Ricardo, claimed that the owners of the means of production extract 'surplus value' from workers by paying them less than the full value of their labour. As with their assaults on speculators, the theme is parasitism; labour and labour alone is the source of the capitalists' excess profit. Critics discern in this, as Parry and Bloch (1989: 4) put it, a 'romantic nostalgia for a world in which production was for use and the interdependence of the human community had not been shattered by exchange'. Marx and Engels' vision harks back to Aristotle's ideal of households as self-sufficient.

Smith's work included praise for the 'minor' virtues of bourgeois life, virtues such as reliability, honesty, hard work, thrift, deferred gratification, punctuality and politeness – the elements of the Weberian Protestant ethic. Essential to the smooth running of *doux commerce*, these virtues were admittedly less heroic than those commended by the Greeks and less self-immolating than those preached by Christian divines. Smith knew that nobler qualities were called for in statecraft, the professions and intellectual life; his point was that the minor virtues, the virtues displayed in everyday exchanges in civil society, were socially useful and not to be despised. But to Marx and Engels, the bourgeois virtues were rank hypocrisy, and Smith's work amounted to a clever apologia for avarice and selfishness. Bourgeois 'virtues' meant a narrow philistinism, foreshadowing the kind of grasping, mean-spirited utilitarianism that Charles Dickens viciously satirized in *Hard Times* through the character of Thomas Gradgrind.

Marx and Engels rejected Smith's account of social order. According to Smith, social order is achieved through market mechanisms; co-ordination without a co-ordinator, guided as it were by an invisible hand, is an orderly system. According to Marx and Engels, capitalism was anarchic. The capitalist market system is not only rapacious and ruthlessly exploitative, it is also prone to recurrent crises that will eventually cause it to crash. They agreed with Smith about the market's dynamism, but disagreed about its implications.

When Marx came across Ricardo's labour theory of value, he saw it as the key to unlock the hidden dynamic of capitalism. The theory postulates that the relative value of goods is determined by the labour time required to produce them. Value derives from the costs of production, and those costs are, ultimately, labour costs. Marx recognized the obvious objection that labour is not the only factor of production: land and capital are also crucial. The labour theory of value accounts for these as the products of *past* labour; thus in Marx's writings capital is often identified as 'dead labour', and capitalists are depicted as 'vampires' who suck the blood of workers, living and dead (Muller 2003: 196–205).

Even at the time he adopted it, the labour theory of value was coming under critical fire; by the 1870s, more and more economists became convinced that the theory was plainly false. In its place they put the theory of marginality as the way to explain not 'value' but *prices* (Slater and Tonkiss 2001: 44–7). In a free competitive market, profit-maximizing firms seek to equate marginal revenue with marginal cost; that is to say, they increase production up to the point where the last unit produced adds the same amount to their income as it does to their costs. This is, happily, the long-term equilibrium state of the market economy.

Two comments are important here. First, marginalist theory explains the so-called 'paradox of value'. Why, in the standard example, are diamonds worth more than water, given that the former are an idle luxury whereas the latter is essential to life? The answer has nothing to do with human folly; the point is that water is abundant (in rich societies!) whereas diamonds are not, with the result that an extra unit of water is worth far less than an extra diamond. Price depends on supply and demand, so goods that are important but in plentiful supply will command a relatively low price compared to scarce goods, however inessential we may judge the latter to be.

Second, Marx's labour theory of value and the marginalist theory of price carry diametrically opposed implications for social equity. Marx argued that capitalism is exploitative because the wages paid to labour are less than the value of that labour; capitalists parasitically extract surplus value from workers past and present. Marginalist theory, conversely, gives a favourable account of prices. The theory implies that consumers pay less than they would be willing to pay for the goods they consume; the difference between these two amounts is the 'consumers' surplus'. If this is so, it means that far from being exploitative the market system delivers us a very good deal.

In contemporary economic texts, the labour theory of value is treated rather like the Ptolemaic theory of the universe: historically interesting, scientifically useless. Tacitly, a growing number of Marxists came to agree with that verdict. A remarkable feature of twentieth-century Marxism is the turn from economic to cultural analysis. This is not to say that the shift was in some sense illegitimate, since culture is at the centre of Marx's own analysis of capitalism. As early as the *Communist Manifesto* of 1848, Marx and Engels wrote: 'Constant revolutionizing of production, uninterrupted disturbance of all social conditions, everlasting uncertainty and agitation distinguish the bourgeois epoch from all earlier ones. All fixed, fast-frozen relations, with their train of ancient and venerable prejudices and opinions are swept away, all new-formed ones become antiquated before they can ossify' (2002/1848: 223). Stable identities cannot form in this constant turmoil; or rather, they coalesce into one identity, the proletariat: 'The bourgeoisie has stripped of its halo every occupation hitherto honoured and looked up to with reverent awe. It has converted the physician, the lawyer, the priest, the poet, the man of science, into its paid wage-labourers' (2002/1848: 222). What is true of occupational and vocational identities is also true of nationality, gender, religion and ethnicity ('race'); all are revealed as illusory. What remains is the reality of class, the development of class consciousness and the contradictions that will bring about the downfall of class society. Twentieth-century Western Marxism was able to drop the discredited labour theory of value without weakening its critique of the capitalist 'free' market.

The Market as Utopia or Dystopia

To its supporters, the free market creates a dynamic society of sovereign consumers who enjoy choice, prosperity and freedom; to its opponents, it produces a dehumanized, unequal society obsessed with commodities and in thrall to transnational corporations.

Table 1.1 Contested features of the market

Pro-market	Anti-market
Choice	Commodity fetishism
Consumer sovereignty	Corporate power
Prosperity	Inequality
Dynamism	Dehumanization
Freedom	Hegemony

Choice versus Commodity Fetishism

The market delivers abundant choice, as a trip to any supermarket will confirm. Take an apparently straightforward product, toothpaste. Consumers can choose between international brands such as Colgate and Macleans, the supermarket's own in-house brand, or cheap 'economy' toothpaste. They can have toothpaste flavoured with freshmint, spearmint or baking soda; toothpaste for sensitive teeth; toothpaste for children; toothpaste for smokers; toothpaste with or without whitener; and toothpaste with or without fluoride. This profusion of choice enables people who are concerned about fluoride to avoid it, people with discoloured teeth to improve their appearance, parents to encourage their children to brush their teeth, affluent people to indulge themselves and poor people to save money.

What is true of mere toothpaste is true of all consumer goods: the market allows us to exercise economic, aesthetic and moral judgements. From this point of view, the more choice we have, the better. Unlike political elections, which occur infrequently and suffer from disappointing rates of participation, voting in the market happens every day and almost everyone takes part (Lindblom 2002: 49). In a political election, citizens typically vote for a party or a candidate, not for individual policies. Governments profess to have a mandate to pursue everything in their manifesto – clearly a false claim, since voters were not able to pick and choose. Buying goods and services, in contrast, is highly specific, because every purchase is a vote for one item and against all the others. The market is truly democratic.

Commodity fetishism, analysed by Karl Marx in the first volume of *Capital*, means that real human relations are pathologically distorted into relations between inanimate objects. It is a form of alienation: we create material objects which take on a life of their own, escaping our control and shaping our lives. We become slaves to our possessions. Culture, a social creation, is turned into something apparently natural and inevitable. A fetishistic focus on commodities obscures the real social relations of production which produced them: the assembly-line, the call centre, the sweatshop. Commodity fetishism serves to depoliticize the capitalist system. The superabundance of trivial choices in the free market is a pathology, not a response to real human needs.

Consumer Sovereignty versus Corporate Power

'Consumption is the sole end and purpose of all production; and the interest of the producer ought to be attended to, only so far as it may be necessary for promoting that of the consumer.' So wrote Adam Smith (1976/1776: 660). The market is a mechanism that functions to ensure that the interests of producers are subordinated to those of consumers. It promotes a competitive struggle in which firms that satisfy their customers will flourish, whereas firms that fail to do so will deservedly be driven out of business. The price mechanism brings this about by incentivizing firms to supply goods and services that customers really want. It follows that the consumer, not the producer, is sovereign.

The critical theorists of the Frankfurt School – notably Adorno, Horkheimer and Marcuse – argued that capitalism entails the manipulation of consumer demand and the creation of what Marcuse (1964) called 'false needs' for consumer goods. The rise of giant transnational corporations, with their ability to control markets and escape regulation by national governments, should shake anyone's faith in the authority of the consumer. Consumer sovereignty is how the system legitimates itself, not how it operates. Capitalism offers bogus cures for the real problems it creates; for example, it produces widespread obesity and thousands of ineffective 'diets' – yielding profits from both.

Prosperity versus Inequality

The free market has delivered more material well-being to more people than any other social system. 'Spending their way towards happiness' is how Lebergott (1993: xi) describes the experience of Americans in the twentieth century. The obvious contrast was with the shoddy products and poor services that were the reality of life under communism.

Although it may be tempting to equate prosperity with crass materialism, there is a case for saying that affluent societies have the potential to create the conditions in which 'people are more cognitively and morally sophisticated, more democratic, more autonomous, healthier, more productive, less materialistic, and happier' (Lane, R. E. 1991: 31). Arguably, it is not prosperity but scarcity that encourages materialistic theories of happiness.

Free marketeers are happy to admit that the market inevitably breeds social inequality. Far from being a problem, this is a corollary of the market's success and should not greatly trouble us. Free markets have raised overall living standards to a degree unimaginable even a century ago. The greatest impact has been not on the rich but the poor, who have been liberated from the wretched conditions and ceaseless drudgery that characterized the lives of earlier generations. The free market requires a mass society of consumers; it cannot flourish merely by satisfying the appetites of the rich. Economic growth 'trickles down' quite quickly from rich to poor – hence the familiar experience of yesterday's luxuries becoming today's taken for granted necessities. A dose of history would be a useful antidote to sentimental nostalgia for pre-industrial society. Nor are rich people parasites; quite apart from the fact that their wealth is a just reward for their success, many of them use it to benefit society as whole – witness the Rockefeller, Ford and Carnegie foundations. Philanthropy, it can be argued, flourishes only under capitalism.

Equality of opportunity is more than compatible with the free market; it is a condition of the market's operation. Equality before God and its secular equivalent, universal human rights, are also completely consonant with the free market. Equality in these senses does not threaten, but expresses, human dignity and liberty. In contrast, the notion of equality of outcome is incoherent, unachievable and disastrous in practice. It violates a fundamental feature of human life, neatly summarized by Adam Smith (1976/1776: 343) as 'the uniform, constant, and uninterrupted effort of every man to better his condition'.

Critics of the free market argue that the social consequences of inequality cannot be disowned so easily. Unless there are checks and balances, free markets create grotesque extremes of wealth and poverty. Even if most people are better off, flagrant disparities of material resources are fateful for the well-being of society as a whole. There is plenty of evidence from the USA and the UK that the policies of neoliberal governments have led to greater inequality, with ghetto communities suffering extreme disadvantage and wracked by crime, violence and drug abuse. Prominent among neoliberalism's growth industries, critics point out, are prisons. Involuntary social exclusion of the disadvantaged is matched by voluntary exclusion of the affluent, who purchase education and health privately, and retreat into affluent neighbourhoods and gated communities.

Dynamism versus Dehumanization

The market is a realm of innovation. Not just new products but new services, new modes of delivery and new forms of organization are perpetually produced in a free market. The economist Joseph Schumpeter called this process 'creative destruction' (Schumpeter 1943). Entrepreneurs who take risks, launching innovative goods and services, are richly rewarded. Firms that sit back and rely on past glory are likely to be severely punished, since customers will desert them.

Workers and unions that resist technological change will find themselves bypassed, like the craft printers whose skills with hot metal were made redundant by the new communication and information technologies.

If consumers are the source of profit whereas workers are counted as costs, then innovations and the competitive struggle will inevitably sacrifice the welfare of workers to that of consumers. However, since most people are producers as well as consumers, this priority of consumption over production is not unequivocally benign in its effects on us.

Max Weber pointed out that the watchword of the market is 'without regard for persons'. To treat people particularistically, according to their relationship to you, is nepotism, a form of corruption. To treat people according to ascribed characteristics such as their age, gender, religion, ethnicity or 'race' is prejudice. The free market, on this view, is the enemy of corruption and prejudice. So far so good, but the price to be paid is dehumanization. The cash nexus dominates social relationships. Our ability to pay, not our need, is what determines the quality of service we receive.

Smart speaks for many critics when he claims that the colonization of ever more areas of social life by impersonal market exchange relations 'has contributed significantly to the increase in indifference shown and ethical disregard displayed towards others in contemporary society' (Smart 2003: 84).

Freedom versus Hegemony

The market requires certain basic freedoms, including freedom of contract and free movement of labour. Markets encourage people to be autonomous, enterprising and self-reliant; markets are thus character-building. Markets cannot function properly if societies prevent their citizens from travelling freely, or if some citizens are unreasonably denied access to certain forms of employment. The market is incompatible with the restrictions imposed by feudal and caste societies. It sweeps away irrelevant distinctions – 'race', for example – and is thus a friend of civil rights.

In market societies there is a tendency for markets to colonize all social relationships. The process may be actively encouraged by governments through programmes to sell off state-owned assets to private enterprise, promote markets or quasi-markets in the public sector, and engineer a culture that will be favourable to the spirit of free enterprise – a so-called 'enterprise culture' (Keat and Abercrombie 1991).

Advocates of the free market often present it as a naturally occurring phenomenon rather than a set of social institutions underpinned by cultural norms and values. It follows from such a view that markets simply need to be set free from political and social constraints; once liberated, the free market will take care of itself, as was expected to happen after the fall of communism. If it is a natural phenomenon, the market can be presented as hard to resist: there is no alternative and you cannot buck market forces, as the communists found out. In any case, the vast majority of people, if we ignore sour puritanical intellectuals, relish the market economy. Hall famously captured the hegemonic project of the Thatcher government in the UK in the phrase 'authoritarian populism' (Hall 1988). The Thatcherite promotion of the free market was passionate, self-righteous and censorious – all characteristics of authoritarianism. Yet, at the same time, Thatcherism was populist, claiming to give ordinary people what they wanted.

Neoclassical economists have been powerful advocates of the market, but they are not alone. Much of the 'cultural turn' in the social sciences, and postmodernist theorizing in particular, can be interpreted as a capitulation of critical reasoning in the face of the dominance of the market. This thesis is advanced by Philo and Miller (2001) in their analysis of contemporary media and cultural studies. The core of their critique is what they identify as an insidious drift towards relativism, epitomized in postmodernist theorizing. Image and being, legend and history, truth and fiction: for relativists these distinctions dissolve into each other. Relativism encourages social scientists to abandon empirical investigation in favour of abstract theorizing. Politics is replaced by irony, and engagement by contemplation. Outside the academy, inequality and deprivation reach new extremes as market forces are unleashed; inside the academy, cultural theorists delight in the playfulness of consumer culture. As academic commentary becomes less and less relevant, investigative journalists carry forward the mission that sociologists have abandoned.

It is not simply that social scientists have been intimidated by new-Right governments or seduced by the research agendas of commercial organizations, though these evils are evident enough. At a deeper level, postmodernist relativism is the ideal complement to the free market. It posits a world peopled by empowered sovereign consumers, whose demands dictate what capitalism supplies, not vice versa. In place of mass culture imposed by a capitalist culture industry with a material interest in selling it to us, we have a rich and resistant popular culture produced by active and knowledgeable consumers. Ironically, as Philo and Miller (2001: 57) comment, 'the "popular" is understood as that which sells a lot or is widely watched. Popular culture is defined in terms of commodities.' Critical social theory has thus been corrupted by the hegemony of the market, a hegemony that would appear to be total.

The Expansion of the Market

For the division of labour fully to develop, markets must expand. The wider the network of people wishing to exchange goods and services, the greater the incentive to specialize. Smith observed that specialization is more highly developed in towns than villages. Efficient means of transport and communication are necessary if markets are to fulfil their potential. Support for free trade between nations was a logical consequence of his recognition of the causal link between the expansion of the market and the division of labour. Here, as throughout *The Wealth of Nations*, Smith's arguments were grounded in his empirical observations of markets in action, and of the ways in which they had expanded over the centuries.

The French historian Fernand Braudel (1992) has provided us with a magisterial account of the rise of the market. His analysis, ably summarized by Slater and Tonkiss (2001: 10–16), traces how marketplaces gradually mutated into and were supplanted by the market. The process involved a number of overlaid transformations:

Place to Space   The marketplace was a focus for a rich variety of social life. People met, made deals, quarrelled, fought, were entertained, and were duly harangued by preachers. The market, in contrast, is an abstract, placeless conceptual field where supply and demand intersect. Marketplaces have no opposite, but the market does; the market is opposed to the plan. This shows that, unlike marketplaces, the market is a counter in a war of ideologies.

Transparent to Opaque   'The primitive market, where food is sold "at first hand" is the most direct and transparent form of exchange, the most closely supervised and the least open to deception' (Braudel 1992: 29). In the marketplace, people can see what they are getting. Buyers are armed with a good practical understanding of produce, fabric, clothing, livestock, tools and similar goods, all of which are part of their fund of common experience. The market, in contrast, is opaque, a point amply demonstrated by the most abstract markets of all, stock markets. Readers of this book are invited to consider what they know about the following financial products: warrants, gilt strips, call options, zero dividend preference shares and perpetual subordinated bonds. Even if such specialized vehicles have little relevance to most people, an uncomfortably high proportion of ordinary savers in the UK have invested in mainstream and apparently low-risk products such as endowment mortgages and with-profits pension plans, only to find them not just opaque but financially ruinous.

Direct to Mediated   A feature of markets, but far less so of marketplaces, is the host of intermediaries who flourish there. In the market the consumer is held to be sovereign; yet if this is so, why are there so many professional advisers turning a good profit? Does it not reflect the opacity of the market?

Regulation to Deregulation   Marketplaces, as Slater and Tonkiss stress, are liminal places, that is to say thresholds that can be crossed by ambiguous characters: 'Foreign merchants – especially members of the great ethnic and familial trading networks, such as Jews and Armenians – come and go, able to escape local surveillance and accountability: they can always disappear into the exotic nowhere land from whence they and their goods appeared' (Slater and Tonkiss 2001: 11). The merchant is a trickster, both an amiable rogue and a callous parasite. Since marketplaces are dangerous they need to be regulated. Ironically, as marketplaces give way to the market the scope for deception increases, yet calls for deregulation grow louder. The need for consumer protection is in inverse proportion to its provision. Caveat emptor, 'let the buyer beware', is a prudent warning in marketplaces, but an ideological dogma of the market.

The historical shifts that Braudel analyses include a move towards impersonality in social relations, a process familiar to sociologists as the transition from *Gemeinschaft* (community) to *Gesellschaft* (association). Even if a great transformation has taken place, it would be a mistake to think that marketplaces have been obliterated. Here is Braudel's verdict on local markets in produce: 'If this elementary market has survived unchanged down the ages, it is surely because in its robust simplicity it is unbeatable – because of the freshness of the perishable goods it brings straight from local gardens and fields. Because of its low prices too . . .' (Braudel 1992: 29). For all the supposed dominance of the abstract market, concrete marketplaces continue to flourish, not least because of popular demand. Without the lived reality of such unbeatable markets and the rich imagery they evoke, 'the market' promoted by neoliberals might lose much of its appeal.

2
Capitalism and the Free Market: Success and Failure

How do advocates of the free market describe and explain its successes and failures? In this chapter, three key ideologies are analysed – market populism, the theory of the efficient market, and market fundamentalism – scrutinizing in each case their response to critiques of the market and their understanding of market failure. I shall argue that the relationship between description (*is*), abstract modelling (*as if*) and prescription (*ought*) is crucial to the legitimation of 'the market' as enjoying the support of the people.

Market Populism

Reflecting on the advantages of co-ordination without a co-ordinator, Friedman (1980: 25) compares the market mechanism to the evolution of a language. The market exists to exchange goods and services, and language exists to exchange ideas and information. Language is a complex structure designed by nobody but created through the multiple interactions of everyone in the community. The words in use, their evolving meanings, and the principles of syntax and grammar arise from social interaction. Only later do authorities seek to codify rules and legislate on anomalies and serious inconsistencies. Even august bodies such as the Académie française are less influential than they appear. The Académie was a late development: it was founded in

1635, just under a hundred years after François I had replaced Latin with French as the legal and administrative language throughout his kingdom. For all its pretensions, Friedman claims, it cannot really legislate correct usage, but simply legitimates changes it is unable to control. If Academicians act against the wishes of ordinary people, their dictates will be ignored, and people will continue to enjoy *le weekend* rather than *la fin de semaine*, and to contact one another *par e-mail* and not *par courrier électronique*.

Surprisingly, Friedman misses the opportunity to highlight the failure of artificial or planned languages. There are hundreds of these, including Volapük (an early example dating from 1879) and Interlingua (launched in 1951). The most famous such language is, of course, Esperanto, developed by Ludwig Zamenhof in the late nineteenth century and spoken by between one and two million people worldwide. Its ideals are lofty: to serve as an international auxiliary language enabling communication between peoples without unfairly imposing one 'ethnic' language such as English as the medium which everyone else must struggle to learn.

As with all such languages, Esperanto is 'rationally' designed. It is grammatically regular, permitting no exceptional cases; spelling is phonetic and consistent; pronunciation is supposedly easy; there are no idioms, such as 'kick the bucket' or 'red herring', whose meaning cannot be deduced from their constituent words; compound words are easily formed out of basic roots; redundancies, such as silent letters and unnecessary accents, are eliminated; and its vocabulary is a hybrid fashioned from words widely recognized in the major European languages. These rational features, it is claimed, make Esperanto quick to learn and easy to use, at least by the favoured Europeans.

Why, then, has Esperanto failed? The truth is that it has not become the international auxiliary language; in most domains, that role is assigned to English. Esperantists attribute this to ignorance, prejudice or cultural imperialism. To the advocates of co-ordination by mutual adjustment, in contrast, planned languages are self-evidently preposterous. How could one person, or a committee, possibly devise a language as rich in meaning as those which have evolved over centuries? Planned languages are like the products of planned economies: inferior. Only an enthusiast could fail to see this, or be surprised at the ridicule Esperanto attracts.

The analogy with natural as opposed to planned languages points to the key claim that the market is democracy in action. New words and constructions are adopted if and only if people vote for them through usage, just as goods and services succeed if and only if people vote for them through purchase. Viewed in this way, the market is a vehicle of democratic consent. Some advocates of the market have taken this interpretation to an extreme position that Frank (2001) has called 'market populism'. Market populists see 'the market' and 'the people' as one and the same. The market is *more* democratic than any of the formal institutions of democracy – elections, legislatures, and government. Political elections take place at long intervals, typically four or five years, whereas purchases are constant. In a political election, people have little or no scope to vote on individual policies, but are forced to vote for or against an entire manifesto; newly elected governments then claim, spuriously, that they have a popular mandate to carry out every policy they set before the electorate. Any purchase we make, in contrast, carries a wealth of detail that manufacturers and retailers take into account in assessing consumer demand and planning new goods and services. The stimulus of competition forces them to be far more sensitive to consumer preferences than any politician need be.

The populist argument that the market is democracy in action contradicts the frequent observation that what the market offers is not 'voice' but 'exit' (Hirschman 1970). In a market, the real power that consumers wield is not so much to complain as to exit by taking their custom elsewhere. Market populists have redefined exit, or voting with one's feet, as the true voice. Their arguments are doubly flawed. First, they misrepresent political democracy, ignoring all the crucial institutions and processes – the ongoing mechanisms of local and national government, political parties, interest groups, voluntary associations, the press, the judiciary, the rule of law, the written or unwritten constitution – that characterize the modern liberal-democratic order. To reduce the meaning of democracy to elections every few years is to trivialize the political process. Electors are citizens whose democratic engagement extends far beyond elections; a healthy democracy depends upon active commitment to the well-being of the republic. On the account offered by market populists, people would be well advised to waste as little time as possible on the political process; apathy would be the rational choice. Second, market populists exaggerate the impact of exit (O'Neill 1998: 99–101), assuming that the mere act of exit necessarily conveys all the information that entrepreneurs need to respond to consumer demand. Exit is presented as invariably a decisive act of rejection, whereas consumers may simply feel it is all they have left when voice is denied. Nor may they have anywhere significantly better to go: for example, they may be dissatisfied with the poor service and meagre rates of interest offered by their bank, yet find exactly the same problems with any other bank they choose. In such a situation there is a high degree of inertia, since if all banks are effectively the same then exit becomes a futile gesture. Market populists' claim that exit is the true voice is simply the ideology of consumer sovereignty crudely restated.

Contemporary glorification of the stock market is a good illustration of market populism in action. Far from needing regulation to ensure democratic accountability, stock markets, it is claimed, should be deregulated so that they can serve the people more effectively. In the 1980s, neoliberal governments promulgated the vision of 'shareholder democracy'. Ordinary people were encouraged to invest in the stock market as a commitment to the capitalist system and as the best means of ensuring the long-term growth of their savings. An iconic case was the Beardstown Ladies (Frank 2001: 131–5), an investment club in the Midwest of the United States. The club's members were mature women whose folksy charm, down-home recipe book and promotional video *Cookin' up Profits on Wall Street* ('learning about investing is as easy as baking an apple pie') was complemented by their apparent ability to outperform the professionals in beating the stock market. (Their claimed investment success was later shown to have been unintentionally inflated.) This warm morality tale demonstrated that the stock market was accessible by ordinary folks, who bought shares in companies whose products and services they knew and used. A happy circle: you and your friends wear Caterpillar work boots because they are hard-wearing; you buy Caterpillar shares because you know the product is good; other people do the same, so the share price rises; you use a populist broker such as Charles Schwab. You, your friends, Caterpillar and Charles Schwab all prosper in this positive sum game for the virtuous. If the market falls there is still good news, since it means an opportunity to buy yet more shares in Caterpillar while they are cheap.

Anti-elitism is a fundamental feature of populist movements. Speaking for an idealized heartland of ordinary people (Taggart 2000), populist leaders rail against the policies and prejudices of intellectual metropolitan elites. As Frank says (2001: 29), the market has 'no place for snobs, for hierarchies, for elitism, for pretence'.

Although it shares this anti-elitist stance, market populism breaks with the populist tradition in two crucial respects. First, populist movements have tended to combine, in various mixes, ethnocentrism, xenophobia and racism. Recent examples of such populism include: in France, Jean-Marie Le Pen's National Front; in Austria, Jörg Haider's Austrian Freedom Party; in Australia, Pauline Hanson's (short-lived) One Nation; and in Italy, Silvio Berlusconi's Forza Italia. In deference to globalization and neoliberal ideology, the Austrian Freedom Party has sought to gain credibility as a modernizing party by embracing carefully selected aspects of globalization, which it represents as a process that can bring Austria *economic*, but not *cultural*, benefits. Such movements pitch their appeal to a people and an indigenous culture that are allegedly threatened by an alien other constituted by its 'race', ethnicity, language or religion – by Jews, Muslims, immigrants, asylum seekers. Market populism tends to free itself from such ethnocentric boundaries, at least symbolically. It appeals, supposedly without prejudice, to 'ordinary people' the world over, an abstract humanity whose desires are taken to be fundamentally the same, always and everywhere. The market claims to liberate us all.

Second, the populist tradition has typically expressed a revolt of small business against giant corporations. A classic French case from the 1950s was Pierre Poujade's Union for the Defence of Shop-keepers and Artisans. His mantle has passed to José Bové's protests against McDonald's and other carriers of American cultural imperialism in the heartland of France. In contrast, market populism presents large corporations as on the side of the people. Corporate leaders such as Rupert Murdoch and Bill Gates are the people's charismatic champions. Market populism paints a world in which entrepreneurs have switched sides, joining the fight against corruption, nepotism, bureaucracy, hierarchy, inherited wealth and cultural elitism. Their and the people's oppressors are the political, cultural and bureaucratic elites, a privileged, public sector 'new class' hostile both to enterprise and the masses. This new class, as Scalmer and Goot (2004) argue in the Australian context, are presented in Murdoch's newspapers as a moral enemy, and, worse still, damned as not real Australians. (Murdoch himself switched from Australian to American citizenship, which helped him to comply with US laws on media ownership.) The new class is funded by taxation and supported by new parasitic industries: the 'welfare industry', the 'Aboriginal industry' and the 'guilt industry' (Cahill 2004). Members of the new class promote their own sectional interests while falsely claiming to be working for the public good.

In keeping with the view that the market is a vehicle of democratic consent, market populists argue that if a corporation enjoys a monopoly it is not an abuse of power but the will of the people. When people protest against monopoly power they are showing disrespect for the ideals of the corporation and the millions of people who support it. European opposition to the US corporate giant Monsanto and its GM crops is interpreted by market populists as an axis of subsidized farmers and food snobs who stand in the way of Monsanto's mission to feed the world. If markets express the will of the people then, as Frank points out, virtually any criticism of business could be described as showing contempt not just for entrepreneurs but also for the common man.

Just as a corporation's market power is interpreted as reflecting the will of the people, so too are the high salaries commanded by corporate executives. They are held to be democratically accountable to shareholders, but in practice private shareholders have no real power. By sleight of hand, corporate executives, who are really bureaucrats, are recast as entrepreneurs. In principle, an entrepreneur is someone who takes risks and reaps the rewards of success or carries the burden of losses; in practice, the corporate executive takes risks with other people's assets, and, win or lose, stands to gain financially.

Market populism flourishes in periods of economic prosperity and booming stock markets, when optimism, naïvety and greed combine to create an illusion of unstoppable progress. The point was made crushingly by J. K. Galbraith in his analysis of the Wall Street crash of 1929. Fraud is closely linked to the business cycle. Galbraith coined the term 'bezzle' to mean the 'inventory of undiscovered embezzlement in – or more precisely not in – the country's businesses and banks' (1961: 152). In boom times, the bezzle is high and undetected, because cash is plentiful and people feel relaxed and contented.

A particularly important point concerns the complicity of accountants and auditors, whose ostensible role is to monitor company accounts and therefore to discover and report on the bezzle. Gerard Hanlon's study of the accountancy profession shows why they fail to do so. As capitalism has moved from Fordism to flexible specialization, accountancy has become increasingly commercialized, particularly in the large firms, who form a self-protecting oligarchy. The global market is dominated by the Big Four: Deloitte Touche Tohmatsu, Ernst & Young, KPMG and PricewaterhouseCoopers. (They used to be the Big Five until the collapse in 2002 of Arthur Andersen, who had failed to uncover Enron's fraudulent accounting practices.) Their clients are neither individuals nor the state, but corporations. They are not neutral as between capital and labour, nor are they vigilant watchdogs of the public interest. Hanlon points to the fissure within the service class, between professions that are bureaucratic or governed by a public service ethos, and those that are profit-oriented servants of capital. The latter are in the ascendant, and accountancy is a leading example. Within accountancy firms, the watchdog role is devalued: 'there has been a decisive shift in terms of prestige and status towards those commercial areas like management consultancy, corporate finance and so on and away from the public spirited, or at least the ambiguously commercial, audit' (Hanlon 1994: 111). Auditing is seen as a bureaucratic waste of time, less profitable than consultancy and unlikely to lead to career progression. To secure lucrative contracts for advice on tax avoidance, corporate finance and management consultancy, accountancy firms regularly quote unrealistically low prices for their audits, thereby giving themselves a financial incentive to conduct audits as quickly and cheaply as possible. Their corporate clients do not complain at this lightness of touch. If price is an index of value, it shows that auditing is of surprisingly little consequence to both its practitioners and its clients. Judged by its results, auditing is about legitimation, not regulation. Thus the accountancy profession has been assimilated into the field of corporate capital.

When the boom goes bust, the extent of the bezzle soon comes to light, as it did after the 1929 crash and after the sudden end of the long boom throughout the 1980s and 1990s. The massive corporate fraud at Enron is emblematic of the process. Major scandals are never uncovered by accountants and auditors; as Galbraith is fond of quipping, 'recessions catch what the auditors missed'. Market populists explain corporate scandals as caused by the rapacity of a minority of corporate executives aided by the laxity of a few incompetent auditors. The fact, however, that they regularly occur in the wake of a slump suggests that the problem is not individual but structural.

The end point of market populism is to hold that the free market is an achieved democratic utopia. Everything that happens, as in Voltaire's satire *Candide*, is for the best in the best of all possible worlds. Such a view is a form of dogma – the dogma known as market fundamentalism. A specific instance of this dogma is the so-called efficient market hypothesis.

The Efficient Market

Until the 1950s, few serious commentators on the world's stock markets would have denied the value of financial analysis in helping investors to identify under-valued shares that represented excellent investment opportunities. Expert analysis could ensure that an investor's portfolio of shares would outperform the stock market, by selecting under-valued shares and avoiding shares that were over-priced relative to their real worth. The assumption was that shares have an intrinsic value that can be determined by investment analysis.

The efficient market hypothesis emphatically denies the validity of this claim. In an efficient market, shares *are* priced at their intrinsic value; there is no such thing as an under- or over-valued share. The reason is that efficient markets have certain key characteristics: there is an abundant flow of information; prices react quickly to changes in information; investors are rational; and deals can be struck quickly and cheaply. According to the hypothesis, Wall Street, the City of London and other leading markets in securities (stocks and shares) fulfil these characteristics amply and are paradigm cases of the efficient market. All the publicly available information about a company is rapidly processed and reflected in movements in the company's share price. The subjective rationalities of all those involved in the market add up to one massive objective rationality. In this situation, there is no rational way to beat the market, since the investor has no information that has not already been factored into prices by the army of analysts and investors that make up the market. Or rather, the only rational basis for attempting to beat the market is if the investor possesses private, price-sensitive information that is not yet in the public domain: advance warning, for example, that a company is about to declare higher profits than expected. Acting on such privileged knowledge – insider dealing – would give the investor an unfair advantage, which is why all the world's major stock markets have strict prohibitions against it. Detecting breaches of these regulations and proving guilt is, of course, difficult, so insider dealing is possibly widespread, probably rational and certainly profitable.

It does not follow from the efficient market hypothesis that investment in the stock market is futile; on the contrary, most financial commentators would say that it is highly profitable, at least in the long run. The correct conclusion is not to abstain from investment nor to try to beat the market, but simply to follow it. The way to do so is to invest in an index fund, one which simply aims to 'track' the market, following its movements up and down as closely as possible.

Within the world of personal financial services the efficient market hypothesis is controversial. It is endorsed by firms marketing index funds, but rejected as preposterous by the managers of actively managed funds that aim to beat the market. (Prudently hedging their bets, many investment houses offer both types of fund.) Is it rational to place one's faith in the rationality of the efficient market? What about the long history of stock market bubbles and crashes, and the documented cases of collective frenzy such as the mania in seventeenth-century Holland for investing in tulip bulbs? Surely a rational actor can profit from these episodes by a 'contrarian' strategy of selling when everyone is buying (thereby avoiding stock market crashes) and buying when everyone is selling (thereby picking up shares when they are cheap)? This would imply that the rational actor can take advantage of bouts of collective irrationality. If so, it means that, for the rational actor, the efficient market hypothesis is a convenient myth.

Market Fundamentalism

In *Globalization and Its Discontents*, Joseph Stiglitz (2002) launches a fierce attack on market fundamentalism. The term fundamentalism is meant to be pejorative. In religion, from which the word is drawn, fundamentalists are people who believe that the sacred text of their faith is without any error whatsoever. In market fundamentalism, the market is treated in the same way. Stiglitz deliberately uses the term to imply zealotry, bigotry and dogmatism. Possessed by a blind faith, market fundamentalists are self-righteous ideologues who will admit no evidence against their position and who refuse to tolerate dissent.

The major institutions promoting market fundamentalism are the International Monetary Fund (IMF), the World Bank and the US Treasury. The policies of these institutions have converged on what Stiglitz calls the 'Washington Consensus'. It has three pillars: *privatization*, selling state-owned assets to the private sector; *liberalization*, deregulating the economy and ending state 'interference' in trade, financial and capital markets; and *austerity*, cutting taxes and slashing government expenditure on welfare and social programmes.

Market fundamentalism has a number of distinctively ideological characteristics:

Refusal of Contrary Evidence   This is, arguably, the key characteristic of market fundamentalism from which all else follows. Stiglitz assembles a battery of evidence to show what has happened when developing countries, including countries in transition from communism, have been forced to follow the dictates of the Washington Consensus. The outcome has been to deepen the gulf between rich and poor; destabilization of the middle class, many of whom emigrate; unemployment; under-investment in education; and bribery, corruption and gangsterism. Ironically, the failure of their policies does not lead market fundamentalists to change their mind. On the contrary, their faith becomes even firmer, which shows the aptness of the religious term, 'fundamentalism'. This is less a scientific theory testable against evidence than a religious dogma immune to any facts.

Fetishism and Reification   Throughout his critique of market fundamentalism, Stiglitz emphasizes the need to examine the impact of specific policies in their wider context. It is a plea to abandon fetishized and reified notions of 'the market' and focus instead on the social realities of markets.

Prescriptivism   Given their fetishized and reified conception of the market, it is logical that fundamentalists should proclaim the free market as the universal solution to social, economic and political problems. Developing societies in search of economic growth, state socialist societies in transition to capitalism, capitalist societies in crisis: no matter what the social context, historical legacy and cultural frame, the market is invariably the panacea.

Hypocrisy   Market fundamentalists are open to the accusation that they recommend to other countries political and economic programmes which they would not adopt for their own country. They preach free trade but practise protectionism.

Denial of Government   In celebrating the market, fundamentalists simultaneously denigrate the role that government plays in regulating the economy. Government action is cast as 'interference'. This is one reason why the Washington Consensus insists that its recommendations are carried out quickly: so that governments do not have the time to obstruct the natural workings of the market. Such profound distrust of government is, paradoxically, politically naïve, since implementation of the Washington Consensus's programmes of privatization, liberalization and austerity is of necessity entrusted to the very governments that are supposedly at the heart of the problem. If a regime is corrupt, trusting it to reform itself is a self-defeating strategy.

Twentieth-century market fundamentalists claim that their programme of minimal government, deregulation and laissez-faire is faithful to the principles set forth in the work of Adam Smith. It is, however, a dubious claim.

Smith emphasized justice as the foundation of liberty. Beneficence, he wrote, 'is less essential to the existence of society than justice. Society may subsist, though not in the most comfortable state, without beneficence; but the prevalence of injustice must utterly destroy it' (Smith 1976/1759: 86). A robust system of law, property rights and morality is essential to market society. So is the infrastructure of roads, railways, canals, bridges and sewers which underpin economic prosperity. So too is a system of public education, without which the division of labour would make people 'as stupid and ignorant as it is possible for a human creature to become' (Smith 1976/ 1776: 782).

It follows that government has a major role to play in putting all this in place. The cause of justice and social order demands numerous exceptions to laissez-faire. Smith strongly supported the Navigation Acts, which, by protecting British shipping from competition and strengthening the Royal Navy, were vital to national prosperity and defence. Similarly, he advocated protectionism if it was undertaken in retaliation against foreign nations' protectionist policies. Again, although opposed to restraints on trade, he recognized the need to protect professional practice from unfettered market forces (Dingwall and Fenn 1987).

Here, as elsewhere in his work, Smith shows himself a practical man of the world. The world's greatest advocate of free trade wrote this: 'To expect, indeed, that the freedom of trade should ever be entirely restored in Great Britain, is as absurd as to expect that an Oceana or Utopia should ever be established in it' (Smith 1976/1776: 471).

As with free trade so with competition: Smith is writing of real humans engaged in competitive struggles with one another. When we turn to the writing of contemporary market fundamentalists, this gritty realism is hard to find, as Backhouse (2002: 327–8) points out in his account of the history of economics. The social reality of markets has been displaced in favour of an abstract fiction: the market.

Market fundamentalists cherish a deep conviction that the free market is always superior to state planning. The collapse of communism provided an opportunity to demonstrate this truth.

In November 1989, shortly after its twenty-eighth anniversary, the German people set about demolishing the Berlin Wall. This momentous event stands as a symbol of the collapse of communism in Central and Eastern Europe. The fall was astonishingly rapid. Czechoslovakia accomplished a peaceful 'velvet revolution' in the same November. Romania's vicious Ceausescu regime was toppled in December. Hungary and Poland became multiparty states in 1990. In Germany itself, monetary and economic union between the Federal Republic of Germany and the German Democratic Republic took place in July 1990, full reunification following in October. The Soviet Union held out only a little longer. Comecon, the communist international trading system, fell apart in January 1991 and was formally disbanded in June. In August of that year, after a failed coup against Gorbachev staged by Soviet hardliners, Boris Yeltsin assumed power and set in motion the break-up of the USSR and Russia's transition to a market economy.

According to one popular economics textbook, 'The year 1989 signalled to the world what many economists had long argued: the superiority of a market-oriented price system over central planning as a method of organizing economic activity' (Lipsey and Chrystal 1999: 3). The events of 1989 were taken to mark the victory not only of the free market but of the intellectual system, neoclassical economics, that enables us to imagine, understand and analyse it. It became possible to see the free market's triumph as the outcome of long-term historical processes of social and intellectual achievement leading to an end state of peace, prosperity, and global democracy – the 'end of history', in Fukuyama's phrase (1992).

Centrally planned command economies are ones in which the allocation of resources and the distribution of income are determined primarily by the decisions of central authorities rather than by market forces. The failure of such economies had tell-tale symptoms for all to see, including:

- *Shortages*: Many goods that consumers wanted remained chronically scarce – famously, in the Soviet Union, toilet paper and soap.
- *Queues*: From time to time, unpredictably, such goods would become available for a brief period, and at an artificially low price. Long queues would rapidly form as the news spread by word of mouth. Willingness to stand in line became the communist equivalent of the capitalist ability to pay. Waiting was largely women's work.
- *Gluts*: Other goods that consumers did not want, such as black-and-white television sets, filled the shops.
- *Shoddy goods*: Goods produced in the Soviet bloc were notoriously inferior, and most could be sold in the West only if they were cheap.
- *Poor services*: Communist officials and service-providers were slow, rude and dismissive. The best their clients could normally hope for was sullen indifference.
- *Pollution*: The countries of the former Soviet bloc have inherited a legacy of environmental degradation unparalleled even in the capitalist West. Low energy costs, the emphasis on heavy industry, inefficient use of resources and a secretive political culture all contributed to the problem. The meltdown of the Chernobyl nuclear reactor was an iconically Soviet disaster: antiquated technology, incompetent management, crude attempts at denial and cover-up.
- *Corruption*: The failings of central planning were in part repaired by semi-legal and illegal trading activities. State property was widely seen as fair game, and taking it was not really stealing. As free marketeers have argued, when everybody owns something, nobody does.

Underlying these symptoms were disturbing structural problems: low labour productivity, obsolescent technologies, faltering economic growth, a bloated military and backward agriculture (Lavigne 1999: 92).

To advocates of the free market, the problems of centrally planned economies can be traced to problems of information.

The first problem is the sheer *quantity* of information that central planners require in order to achieve an efficient alloca- tion of resources. In practice they can never come near acquir- ing the information they need, so their decisions are inevitably based on hopelessly inadequate data. Whether they could process all the data if they had it is doubtful – but the problem will never arise.

Even more intractable is the second problem, the *quality* of information. Data are supplied to central planners by enterprises that then become the subject of the planners' edicts. The result is inescapable: firms will cheat. They will give to the planners false or doctored information, to buy themselves a quieter, more manageable life. Even though the central planners may know this to be the case, there is little they can do about it. If they try to correct the data they are given, firms will respond by supplying even falser figures in future. More bureaucracy, more regulation, more falsifica- tion, more bureaucracy. For Lavigne (1999: 12) it was this vicious circle that made the Soviet system incapable of reforming itself, rendering its ultimate defeat by free market capitalism inevitable.

The poor quality of the information that circulates in a command economy points to a third problem, one repeatedly emphasized by Hayek. Much of the information needed if an economy is to function efficiently is not consciously theorized and cannot be codified. Instead, it is embodied in practical, locally grounded knowledge of people, conditions and special circumstances, a type of knowledge that expresses itself in practical skills, habits and dispositions. Hayek argued that it is precisely this kind of knowledge that entrepreneurs possess and exploit. It lies totally beyond the reach of central planners.

Sociological studies of work and industry have consistently demonstrated the importance of such 'tacit' knowledge and the skills associated with it. A powerful recent example is Strangleman's (2004) study of the railway industry in the UK, which shows how, legitimized by the neoliberal strategy to break the power of the unions and privatize the industry, man- agement sought systematically to destroy the autonomous workplace culture that had played such a key role in making the railway system work. Management's aim was to sweep away the store of cultural knowledge, values and dispositions that had been transmitted from generation to generation, replacing it with top-down job specifications and an arsenal of surveillance and discipline – a classic formula of command and control. The new managers were just that: managers, not railway men. They had no prior experience of the industry, and held its customs and practices in some contempt. Examples like this show the vulnerability of Hayek's argument, as O'Neill points out (1998: 138–42). For Hayek, only the free market system can exploit the potential of tacit knowledge; but surely markets, particularly in an era of globalization, tend to obliterate the knowledge possessed by weak and marginalized actors – indigenous peoples, peasants, 'deskilled' workers. It may be that command economies cannot take advantage of tacit knowledge; but that does not prove that markets necessarily do so either, and is therefore not a valid argument for market fundamentalism.

When communism crumbled, the Washington Consensus urged what Stiglitz calls 'shock therapy' or the 'big bang' approach. Partly this was through fear that, unless change were rapid, the communists might seize power again. The old state bureaucracies would inevitably be opposed to market forces, and had to be bypassed because they were part of the problem, not the solution. There was a pressing need to create, as swiftly as possible, new classes of entrepreneurs and consumers with a stake in the market system.

The Washington Consensus holds as an article of faith that markets arise quickly and spontaneously in response to demand. The transition from communism to the market system was seen less as a matter of building institutions than of demolishing obstacles. All the reforms were to be implemented simultaneously – which, ironically, implied a massive feat of social engineering. The Soviet Union and its satellites had themselves made repeated attempts at reform: after Stalin's death in 1953; in the 1960s; and in the 1980s, with Gorbachev's *perestroika*. Terminology associated with the market system began to be deployed in command economies, leading to excessive optimism in the West about the prospects for reform. As Lavigne argues (1999: 41), simply because the command economies *talked* of prices, profits, interest rates and efficiency, Western experts tended to assume that dismantling central controls would rapidly allow market adjustments to the new realities of supply and demand. Although this proved to be an illusion, the dogma of market fundamentalism remained intact, demonstrating its capacity to withstand evidence of its failure.

Public Choice Theory

'Public choice theory' is the rather unhelpful name for a body of work that aims to apply economic analysis to the field of political life in general, and specifically to the activities of politicians, voters and bureaucrats. As we shall see, public choice theory was a useful resource for the project of neoliberal social reconstruction that was set in train in a number of Western societies from the late 1970s onward.

A crucial feature of free-market thinking, as Smart (2003: 112–15) emphasizes, is the assumption that people are motivated primarily by self-interest *in all domains of social life*. Applying this view to politics leads to profound scepticism about the ideals of 'public service' touted by politicians, civil servants and professional associations. The public sector, on this view, is not characterized by an ethos of public service, and those employed in it are not altruistic 'knights' but self-interested 'knaves'. Public choice theory has, it soon becomes clear, a strongly cynical quality.

Public choice theory claims to be universal in scope. The reason is simple: the theory allegedly reflects the reality of human nature. Most people are at most times and in most situations self-interested; at best, their altruism is strictly limited. Advocates of the free market recognize this truth, and work with rather than against the grain of human nature. Even if they concede that public spirit plays some part in political life, public choice theorists warn us not to base social policy on the assumption that people will behave altruistically. It is far safer to assume the opposite, and to adopt a precautionary principle in designing social institutions. This point is put succinctly by O'Neill (1998: 172): 'The problem of the vulnerability of institutions to the vicious, the egoist, the careerist, and the lover of lucre and power, are problems that any plausible social and political theory has to take seriously.'

Realistic appraisal of the motivations of politicians and state bureaucrats should not be allowed to become a monopoly enjoyed by public choice theorists. The same scepticism, as O'Neill points out, is to be found in Marx's critique of Hegel. Under capitalism, the state bureaucracy is not a disinterested body standing above civil society, but a part of civil society that ruthlessly pursues its own interests. The crucial difference is that Marx focuses on the workings of the capitalist social order and the culture it produces, whereas public choice theorists put forward what purport to be universal truths derived from human nature and therefore applicable to all cultural settings. Hence public choice theory assumes that individual preferences precede and explain institutional arrangements. Consumers naturally seek to acquire goods, politicians naturally seek votes, and bureaucrats naturally seek career advancement.

Public choice theory is a particular and not very subtle variant of rational choice theory, which we shall examine in the following section. It adopts a crude view of motivation, in which, as O'Neill remarks, politicians are merely hacks and bureaucrats merely careerists. Such a blanket view prevents us from drawing any distinctions between them; all are equally guilty of the basest egoism.

The cynical, debunking attitude to public officials was unmistakable in the neoliberal project of social reconstruction. If, in Le Grand's words (2003), the British welfare state from 1945 to 1979 was an era of 'knights rampant', the year 1979, when Margaret Thatcher came to power, ushered in 'the triumph of the knaves'. The post-war period to 1979 appeared to be a golden age of welfare. Policy-makers and civil servants were perceived to be competent and benevolent, professional practitioners were manifestly motivated by high ideals of service to clients and the community, and, crucially, taxpayers were thought to be willing to pay for the welfare state. As for people receiving welfare, they were seen as deferential to experts in authority and happy with a standardized basic service that was free to all at the point of delivery.

To its neoliberal critics, the golden age of welfare was a golden age of bureaucracy, inefficiency, dependency and featherbedding. As the golden age wore on, so its critics said, the problems became more acute: not just bureaucrats and civil servants, but also professionals, were the target of wide-spread disillusionment and distrust; ever larger sections of the middle class opted out of state provision into the private sector; and 'tax and spend' policies were widely repudiated, particularly when they had income redistribution as a goal.

If it is assumed that workers are knaves and consumers ought to be sovereign, the obvious thing to do in order to deliver public services efficiently and effectively is, as Le Grand remarks (2003: 9), to unleash the power of the market. In sectors where full privatization was rejected as unachievable or undesirable, the government created 'quasi-markets'. In these markets, the state provides the finance, typically appointing a purchasing agent to act on behalf of the consumer; on the supply side, non-profit or even publicly owned agencies compete for custom.

Although such quasi-markets have been severely criticized by the Left, Le Grand defends the principle behind them. The various proposals he puts forward aim to secure the benefits of the market, not least the empowerment of consumers, while mitigating some of the drastic consequences that full marketization can bring, above all gross inequalities of wealth and power. He argues that it is possible to devise mechanisms that secure the same desired actions from knights and knaves alike. 'This can be achieved', he claims (Le Grand 2003: 168), 'by systems that offer personal (or institutional) rewards for activities that are perceived to benefit users, but for which the rewards are not so great as to eliminate any sense of personal sacrifice that is associated with the activity concerned'. Egoists and altruists will both be encouraged to perform the same desirable actions for the good of consumers. Managed properly, quasi-markets are a form of *doux commerce publique* (see chapter 1, p. 17). They have the considerable merit of promoting respect for people who rely upon welfare systems.

Rational Choice and Instrumental Rationality

Market populism and market fundamentalism are two ideologies regularly deployed to legitimize policies of deregulation, privatization and austerity in the public sector. Their counterpart in the academic sphere is rational choice theory. Like them, it is controversial.

Rational choice theory has a number of defining features, of which two are key. First, it is committed to methodological individualism, the principle that social phenomena can and should be reduced to the characteristics of individual human beings. Firms, trade unions, governments and the nation-state are abstractions; on this view, society is no more than the sum of its individual members. From this follows the economist's characteristic reliance on aggregate statistics. Second, rational choice theory holds that people normally act so as to achieve their goals in the most efficient way they can in the light of their preferences and knowledge. Taken together, these two features mean that social order is not a matter of custom, tradition or shared values, but an equilibrium brought about by countless mutual adjustments among calculating, rationally oriented individuals.

Many commentators have noted a polarization between the advocates of rational choice theory and its opponents. This is also an obvious disciplinary gulf, with economics as the bastion of rational choice theory and the other social sciences as its detractors. Anyone seeking a compromise, such as Beckford (2000), has to show extreme caution. Although he is quite right to say that each side is fighting against a caricature of its enemy, the war is real enough. Rational choice theory builds abstract theoretical models unashamedly based on brutally simplifying assumptions, deducing propositions from axioms and confidently asserting their predictive power. Other varieties of social theory are typically more eclectic and messy, insisting on the particularities of the social and cultural context, inductive rather than deductive, and wary of prediction. The distinction is neatly captured in the contrast between the 'clean models' of economics and the 'dirty hands' of sociology (Hirsch et al. 1996).

Rational choice theory is not, however, homogeneous. Goldthorpe (1998) has cogently set out three dimensions on which various formulations of rational choice theory can be ranged.

Strong/objective or Weak/subjective Rationality?   Very few advocates of rational choice theory would argue that

actors' goals must be rational. Instead, they take goals as given, and treat rationality as applying to the means people select to achieve their goals. Neoclassical economic theory typically postulates that actors have perfect knowledge of all relevant information available, so that they make an objectively optimal choice of means. Some economists, and most other practitioners of rational choice theory, adopt a weaker version of rationality, one which requires that actors have subjectively good reasons for their choices, without implying that their knowledge is perfect.

Situational or Procedural Rationality?   Mainstream economics sees rationality as a logical reaction to a situation; it is profoundly uninterested in the psychology of decision-making. Theorists who adopt a subjective view of rationality are more likely to be drawn to consider the psychological procedures through which decisions are reached. Interestingly, Goldthorpe himself argues strongly that a situational view of rationality is more productive for sociology, and that sociologists should have little concern for psychological processes or mental states. As we shall see in chapter 3, this would preclude consideration of an immense body of social-psychological findings on human 'irrationality', findings which have profound implications for sociological critiques of market society.

A General or a Specific Theory of Action?   One approach to rational choice theory is to regard it as applying to a delimited field of social life, such as the pursuit of material desires through economic exchange in the market. Most advocates of rational choice theory are, however, not content to confine their ambitions to 'the economy' as an insulated domain, as though it could be compartmentalized. Rational choice theory tends to be imperialistic; its practitioners seek to colonize the whole of social science, a characteristic amply displayed in Becker's *The Economic Approach to Human Behaviour* (Becker 1976), which addresses crime and punishment; marriage, fertility and the family; the allocation of time between work and leisure; the operation of democracy; and discrimination based on 'race'. According to Becker, the economic approach is uniquely powerful, and offers *the* unifying theoretical framework that was sought but not discovered by great social theorists such as Comte (in positivism), Bentham (in utilitarianism) or Marx (in socialism). No aspect of life lies beyond the reach of rational choice theory, not even the realm of the sacred, which has been analysed by Stark and Bainbridge (1987) in their book, *A Theory of Religion*.

Goldthorpe argues for a version of rational choice theory that would be specific rather than general. Even so, he claims that it is a 'privileged' theory: 'not just one theory of action among others but rather *the* theory with which attempts at explaining social action should start and with which they should remain for as long as possible' (Goldthorpe 1998: 184). It is unlikely that his attempted compromise will attract rational choice theory's opponents, representing as it does an only lightly modified form of imperialism.

To its critics, the portrait of humanity, conventionally known as *homo economicus* or economic man, is self-evidently absurd. We know from experience and introspection that rational calculation is only one aspect of the human condition. The great sociologist Max Weber recognized this. Much of our action is governed by emotions; some of it is habitual behaviour; and some is fired by political, ethical or religious ideals, which can produce acts of altruistic self-sacrifice.

Advocates of rational choice theory have two basic lines of counter-attack to the charge that their model of humanity is hopelessly lopsided. One is to argue that *homo economicus* is an accurate picture, even if we find it difficult to acknowledge. On this view, our vaunted ideals, our personal attachments, even our altruism, are rooted in self-interest. This is the justification for rational choice theory's imperialistic ambitions, but it is a position that can easily degenerate into tautologies. The fact that we choose to act altruistically shows that we derive satisfaction from altruism, hence our altruism is not pure but self-interested; and so on. The self-interested character of human action ceases to be an empirical proposition and becomes, uninterestingly, true merely by definition. As Slater and Tonkiss comment (2001: 61), *si omnia nulla*: if it explains everything, it explains nothing.

A second line of defence is the claim that rational choice theory is valid because it yields accurate predictions. Never mind whether or not it captures the human psyche; it works. Its descriptive accuracy is irrelevant. Instead, it is concerned solely with the predictive power of *as if* assumptions. In the philosophy of science, this is the position known as instrumentalism. Scientifically postulated entities such as neutrinos or quarks are not 'real', but theoretical terms that assist explanation and prediction. The classic source for this position in economics is Milton Friedman's *Essays in Positive Economics* (1953). To criticize rational choice theory on the ground that its assumptions are 'unrealistic' is to misunderstand the status of theoretical terms. On this view – to which we shall return in chapter 3 – the abstract quality of rational choice theory is not a defect, but its glory.

Rational choice theory implies that the social world is governed by the principle that Weber termed *Zweckrationalität*, usually translated as goal-rationality or instrumental rationality. Weber wrote (1964/1922: 117):

> Action is rationally oriented to a system of discrete individual ends (*zweckrational*) when the end, the means, and the secondary results are all rationally taken into account and weighed. This involves rational consideration of alternative means to the end, of the relations of the end to other prospective results of employment of any given means, and finally of the relative importance of different possible ends. Determination of action, either in affectual or in traditional terms, is thus incompatible with this type.

Instrumental action is based on a rational calculation of the best means to achieve any given end. As Weber makes clear, it is incompatible with action derived from an emotional response, and with action taken in accordance with what tradition requires. Nor is it compatible with what Weber called *Wertrationalität*, value-oriented action, which involves 'a conscious belief in the absolute value of some ethical, aesthetic, religious, or other form of behaviour, entirely for its own sake and independently of any prospects of external success' (Weber 1964/1922: 115).

Value-oriented action is always motivated by the fulfilment of unconditional demands. Unlike instrumentally rational action, it is unconcerned with costs and consequences, which means that in extreme cases it can take the form not only of self-sacrificing altruism but also of ruthless, inhumane actions by zealots, fanatics and terrorists. It might be thought that, by contrast, instrumentally rational action, however unheroic and self-centred, is at least relatively harmless. In his dictionary of economics, Black (1997: 136–7) defines 'economic man' as follows:

> A person who is entirely selfish and entirely rational. While such a person in pure form is a caricature met only in economic models, there is a sufficient element of this in enough people to make economic models relevant to real life. Real people are in various ways both better and worse than economic man. Economic man may only obey laws because of the penalties for being caught, and only keep bargains from concern for his reputation, but he is free from malice and dogmatic resistance to change.

Weber and his descendants take a less favourable view of instrumentally rational economic actors. A leading example is Jürgen Habermas, who emphasizes the amoral nature of instrumental rationality together with the fact that it is becoming dominant in our lives; in his phrase, it is 'colonizing the life-world'. Modern societies are increasingly technocratic.

Among the most powerful critiques of instrumental rationality is Zygmunt Bauman's devastating analysis of the Holocaust (Bauman 1989). His thesis strikes against the optimistic view that European history since the Enlightenment is a triumph of reason over superstition. He rejects grand narratives of history such as the promise that psychoanalysis will tame our animal nature, and the claim that Marxism is the science of liberation from oppression.

For Bauman, the Holocaust was not an atavistic reversion to barbarism. The Final Solution did not depend on recruiting psychopaths or unleashing the mob to commit irrational brutality. Its success came not from mobilizing hatred but from neutralizing human feelings. It put people – perpetrators, collaborators, witnesses and victims – into situations where they were forced to be instrumentally rational. People were constantly presented with choices: how to save yourself, whether you could rescue others, and if so, which others, how many, and at what risk? Bauman reports a characteristic episode. Fourteen inmates of the concentration camp at Sorbibór attempted to escape but were captured. Before being shot they were ordered each to choose another victim to die with them. They refused. The commandant announced that unless they chose, he would personally select fifty people to be executed. They chose; on what basis, Bauman does not speculate. Here is a real-life situation, repeated with countless variants throughout the Third Reich; life and death choices subject to an instrumentally rational calculus.

Bauman emphasizes the modernity of Nazi racism. Of course, anti-semitism has a two-thousand-year pedigree in Christian cultures. Jews were Christ-killers, but they could be redeemed from sin by conversion to Christianity. Under Nazism, Judaism was not the issue, Jewishness was. Hitler's own outpourings were riddled with metaphors of disease, infection, infestation, putrefaction and pestilence. Jews were bacilli, viruses, decomposing germs. The Final Solution evolved into a project to cleanse the world of vermin. As Bauman argues, the imagery of 'race' gave legitimacy to the project of genocide. 'Racial' inferiority was constructed as an incurable plague that had to be destroyed before it propagated itself. The Final Solution depended upon distinctively modern, scientific conceptions, including medical metaphors of health, pathology, hygiene, sanitation and surgery. Anti-semitism in Nazi Germany was a form of social engineering in pursuit of a warped utopia.

Bauman's thesis has been heavily criticized, most notably by Yehuda Bauer (2002), who argues that Bauman underplays the part played by the ideology of anti-semitism. True, most Germans were not murderous anti-semites; many were, however, 'moderately' anti-semitic and quite content to see the Jews removed from positions of power and influence in German society. This form of anti-semitism was not unique to Germany but widespread throughout Europe; what was distinctive to the German case was the capture of power by a Nazi elite of lethally anti-semitic pseudo-intellectuals, propelled by the bogus science of 'race' and a perverted vision of a 'racially' cleansed Reich, and supported by large sections of the scientific, professional and cultural intelligentsia. Genocidal anti-semitism was a top-down process, but it could not have prevailed without the collusion of grass-roots 'moderate' anti-semitism.

It is also true, as Bauer points out, that the Nazi bureaucratic system was an assembly of incompetent, inefficient and faction-ridden fiefdoms. This truth is not, however, damaging to Bauman's case. The instrumental rationality of a bureaucracy – calculative, rule-bound, dispassionate – is no guarantee of efficiency. Bauman's key point is nothing to do with efficiency; it is, rather, to insist on the modernity of the Holocaust, rejecting any easy explanation that seeks to limit its significance by treating it either as a uniquely German phenomenon or as simply an instance of a long-standing Christian reflex. Bauman urges us to confront the terrible conclusion that the Holocaust 'was born and executed in our modern rational society, at the high stage of our civilization and at the peak of human cultural achievement, and for this reason it is a problem of that society, civilization and culture' (Bauman 1989: x).

As Weber argued, the institutional carrier of instrumental rationality is the modern, rationally organized bureaucracy. Bureaucracy is animated by a rational spirit, the spirit of technical efficiency, good design, obedience to rules, hierarchy, the application of objective science and the relegation of values to the realm of subjectivity. As in rational choice theory, goals are not interrogated but taken as given; all the focus and effort is devoted to the means to achieve the goals. Hence the supreme irony that, even as the war was being lost, and when Hitler's armed forces were desperate for infrastructure, munitions and reinforcements, the bureaucratic machinery of the Holocaust proceeded unchecked in its task of eliminating Jews from an empire that was on the point of surrender.

The opponents of rational choice theory should take it seriously. It is, after all, a constituent part of the social reality which it seeks to explain. Many policy-makers and advisers have been trained in rational choice theory, and try, at least in part, to put it into practice. The thrust is to destroy collective solidarity and bolster individualism (Archer and Tritter 2000: 15). Armed with rational choice theory, decision-makers seek quantified measures of individual output and productivity. In the world of work, this has created an apparatus of appraisal, target-setting, monitoring, payment by results and destruction of collective bargaining; as Bourdieu puts it, 'methods of rational control which, while imposing over-investment in work . . . combine to weaken or destroy collective references and solidarity' (Bourdieu 1998b: 97–8).

A theme of this book is that, as Beckford says (2000: 229): 'social and cultural life in advanced industrial societies has evolved in a symbiotic relation with prevailing social science theories because they have all been influenced and shaped by the forces that gave rise to forms of modernity, including its ambiguities and contradictions'. If we want to analyse contemporary understanding of individuality, rationality, freedom, choice, modernity and the market, we need to inter-rogate and critique the theory of rational choice – 'the grand theory of high modernity' (Archer and Tritter 2000: 1).

If there is a total war between rational choice theory and its enemies, the question presumably arises for all of us, 'Whose side are you on?' More generally, 'Are you for or against the market?' Neutrality is, it appears, impossible. Yet there is a pro-found paradox here. On the one hand, the market is tri-umphant: markets have expanded to cover the globe; the major alternative to the capitalist market economy, communism, has collapsed; Marxism appears to be exhausted; neoliberal gov-ernments have introduced market principles into sectors hith-erto insulated against them; market populism is a dominant ideology in capitalist societies; market fundamentalism is a dogma successfully imposed on the Third World and societies in transition from communism; economics reigns supreme in the social sciences, and has even infiltrated its great enemy, soci-ology. On the other hand, the market meets fierce resistance: from anti-globalization movements; from the Greens; from the Left; from societies that have suffered from the recipes of market fundamentalists; and from all those outside economics who reject the portrait that reduces human beings to 'economic man'. Rational choice theory has the curious feature that it is both imperialistic and iconoclastic. Economists still have to struggle to convince others that co-ordination by mutual adjust-ment, co-ordination without a co-ordinator, is even feasible, let alone desirable. Paradoxically, faith in the market is simultane-ously an established orthodoxy and a subterranean heresy.

Market Failure

Most advocates of the market allow for the possibility of market failure. A market fails, in their perspective, when its performance is significantly poorer than the most efficient outcomes that could be achieved. A market may fail to produce goods and services that are in demand, or produce goods and services that few people want, or distribute resources in an inefficient way.

To critics who are sceptical of the market, what market failure shows is that, quite literally, markets can fail; the market does not work well in all social situations. To advocates of the free market, the conclusion is very different: the cause of market failure is not the market itself but market 'imperfections'. Because of these imperfections, particular markets may fail, but the market as an ideal remains intact.

Not only is the interpretation of market failure contentious; even identifying instances of market failure is not so straightforward as some textbooks imply. This is because market failure, to free marketeers, has a strict meaning. Market failure occurs when prices fail to reflect the full social costs and benefits of activities. Market failure means a falling short of economic efficiency, that is the state of an economy in which no one can be made better off without someone being made worse off (the Pareto optimum). It does not mean a situation judged to be politically, socially or ethically undesirable.

Take, for example, the question of so-called 'merit goods'. These are goods and services whose consumption is held to be so beneficial to society as a whole that people must be compelled to consume them. Left to their own devices, many people, it is feared, would under-consume these goods. The standard case is education. Young people might prefer to leave school as soon as possible in order to seek a full-time job; a goal that may be shared by parents, including the self-employed who want children to assist and eventually succeed them in the family business. The notion that some children, especially girls, need to be taught only the basics of reading, writing and arithmetic, has some populist appeal. Recognizing that education is a merit good, people throughout the civilized world are compelled by legislation, whether they wish it or not, to arrange education for their children at least up until the national school-leaving age.

Only the most extreme free marketeers would argue against compulsory education. Even so, conflicts about the content of the national curriculum, and disputes about the benefits of higher education, show that the case for education as a merit good is not straightforward. The concept of merit goods breaches the principle of consumer sovereignty. Free marke-teers fear that merit goods can serve to justify the imposition by political elites of their own tastes for 'high' culture, or their own recipes for how the masses ought to live their lives. This is the route, the free marketeers say, to the grotesque policy of subsidizing extravagant opera houses that only the affluent can afford to attend. To free marketeers, merit goods are really an example of positive externalities – and these, as we shall see below, can be handled perfectly well within a free market framework.

Even more contentious than merit goods is the issue of extremes of wealth and poverty. Let the market rip, and such extremes will inevitably result. When countries such as the USA and the UK introduced neoliberal policies in the 1980s and 1990s, disparities of wealth and income rose sharply. As with merit goods, some advocates of the free market are prepared to treat this as a market failure, but many others are not. It was, to recapitulate a point made in chapter 1, a central concern of Adam Smith's *Wealth of Nations*. Modern com-mercial societies create greater inequalities than did, say, feu-dalism; but the vast majority of people are far better off under a market system. Inequality is the price that has to be paid for economic efficiency and freedom, and shows not the failure of the market but its success.

In addition to the controversies surrounding merit goods and inequality, the literature recognizes four main sources of market failure: monopoly, lack of information, externalities and public goods. Even here there are doubts about the reality of such problems. Where the problems are acknowledged, the crucial issue is to decide whether the solution involves working with or against the grain of the market.

Monopoly   Adam Smith put the case against monopoly with classic simplicity. 'The monopolists, by keeping the market con-stantly under-stocked, by never fully supplying the effectual demand, sell their commodities much above the natural price . . . The price of monopoly is upon every occasion the highest which can be got' (1976/1776: 78). To operate effectively, the market requires consumer sovereignty: 'Consumption is the sole end and purpose of all production' (1976/1776: 660). In a famously cynical remark, Smith argues that firms will seek to restrict competition if they can: 'People of the same trade seldom meet together, even for merriment and diversion, but the conversation ends in a conspiracy against the publick, or in some contrivance to raise prices' (Smith 1976/1776: 145).

Where one supplier captures a market (monopoly), or where a few suppliers succeed in restricting competition (oligopoly), goods and services will be under-supplied and over-priced. The power of a monopoly derives from the fact that demand for its product is inelastic, so that it can raise its prices without significantly losing sales. If there is no competition from new entrants to the industry, costs will tend to drift upwards. Monopolies are against the public interest, since they prosper to the detriment of consumers.

Lack or Asymmetry of Information   For markets to work efficiently, people need to be fully informed about the goods and services they are buying or selling. No real market lives up this ideal; information is never complete, and there is often a significant asymmetry, with sellers knowing more than buyers, or vice versa.

The market for professional services is often cited as an instance where information asymmetry favours sellers. Lay people simply cannot feasibly acquire the level of knowledge possessed by doctors, lawyers, accountants and so on. This opens up the possibility that professional people can exploit the situation, charging excessive fees for services that were poor quality or not really needed. What, other than a commitment to professional ethics, will prevent them from exploiting their clients?

If consumers do not have sufficient information on which to base their choices, inferior goods and services will tend to drive out superior ones. Akerlof's (1970) famous example is the market for second-hand cars. People selling cars know a great deal about the car's history, and whether it has been reliable or troublesome. Conversely, the people buying cars will find it difficult, at the point of purchase, to distinguish the good cars from the 'lemons'; the easiest way to find out is by happy or bitter experience. If consumers have literally no way of distinguishing a good car from a bad one, the price of all the cars will be the same. Someone with a good car for sale will not be able to charge a higher price for it, and someone selling a lemon will have no reason to drop the price. Ironically, good cars will be underpriced and poor cars overpriced. People with good cars will hold on to them; people with lemons will try to sell them as soon as they can. Bad cars will drive out the good.

The insurance industry provides examples of an asymmetry where buyers have the advantage over sellers. If insurance cover is equally open to anyone, it will be most attractive to the people who are most at risk, since they are the ones most likely to profit from it. Health insurance will be attractive to people who know they are in poor health; people in good health will be subsidizing the unhealthy, an instance of the problem known as *adverse selection*. It is in the interest of healthy people to avoid unselective schemes and secure more favourable terms from a specialist insurer who demands a medical examination.

Externalities   Economic efficiency requires that producers bear all the costs of production and their customers gain all the benefits of consumption; costs and benefits are 'internalized' within the exchanges between buyers and sellers. Resources are used efficiently because the social costs and benefits of activities are fully reflected in the prices paid for them. Externalities occur when this is not so, that is when third parties are either disadvantaged by or benefit from transactions between other buyers and sellers.

A negative externality (an external diseconomy) occurs when producers or consumers are able to pass the costs of their activity on to others; for example, when car manufacturers avoid paying the full cost of traffic congestion and exhaust pollution. External costs are not reflected in prices, so goods are underpriced, oversupplied and overconsumed; from the standpoint of economic efficiency, cars will be too cheap and there will be too many of them.

Conversely, a positive externality (an external economy) occurs when producers or consumers do not gain the full benefit of their enterprise; instead, other people benefit without bearing the cost. If 93 per cent of the population is immunized against measles, mumps and rubella, the population enjoys 'herd immunity'; hence the remaining 7 per cent need not run the risk of side effects from immunization, but can take a 'free ride' on the efforts of their fellow citizens. External benefits are not reflected in prices, so goods are overpriced, undersupplied and underconsumed. In the UK at the time of writing, the take-up of the combined measles, mumps and rubella vaccine has, owing to fears about possible side effects, fallen below the 93 per cent level required for herd immunity.

Public Goods The market economy deals most effectively with what some economists call 'normal' goods. These are the array of items that are typically for sale in a modern economy: bananas and camcorders, books and hamburgers, guns and butter. Consumers purchase them at a price, and assume ownership over them. What consumers then do with the items they have bought is entirely up to them within the limits of the law; so a consumer who throws away a hamburger in disgust, or in protest against cultural imperialism, has still, from the economic point of view, consumed it.

Normal goods have two crucial properties. They are *excludable*, in the sense that other people can be prevented from using them. The banana I have purchased is my property; I have rights over how it is used. Normal goods are also *rivalrous*, in the sense that the amount one person consumes reduces the amount that others can consume; I have just bought the last bunch of bananas in the greengrocer's.

Public goods are the exact opposite of normal goods. They are *non-excludable*, that is, once they have been supplied nobody can be prevented from enjoying the benefits: for example, clean air and national defence. Non-excludable goods are common property; no person, organization or country has property rights over them. In a free market, the tendency is for these goods to be over-used. Common land becomes barren, and wildlife is shot to extinction. Public goods are also *non-rivalrous*, in that one person's enjoying them does not prevent others from doing so, at least until capacity is reached. Amenities such as art galleries, museums, parks, roads and bridges, are non-rivalrous. People can be charged for using them, but it may not be worth the trouble, and will have the effect of excluding poorer people. In such cases the amenity will be underused. To avoid this, many people argue that they should be free – or, more precisely, that they should be charged at zero price at the point of consumption. How, then, can a private company sell them? If it were left to the market, public goods would be under-supplied or, in many cases, not supplied at all. Instead they are typically financed either by altruistic voluntary activity or by taxation.

Denying Market Failure: In Defence of Monopoly

Merit goods and social inequality may not signify as market failures; but surely monopoly is unquestionably damaging to the free market? The classic work of Adam Smith, and countless economics textbooks, underline the apparently obvious fact that monopolies are anti-competitive. Monopolists can cream off excess profits and, protected from competition, can continue to supply inferior goods and services. Monopoly is a major cause of market failure.

Yet we have also seen, earlier in this chapter, the contrary argument of the market populists: that firms and their products achieve market dominance because consumers vote for them with their purchases. In Emerson's dictum, these firms have built 'a better mousetrap'. On this interpretation, campaigns for strict anti-trust legislation are ideologically driven by populist hostility to big business.

That is the case advanced by Bork in *The Antitrust Paradox* (1993). For him, anti-trust legislation serves a useful social purpose only when it promotes competition and free entry to open markets. Throughout the book he emphasizes that maximization of consumer welfare is the only legitimate goal of anti-trust laws in a free society. Departure from this principle has embroiled the judiciary in politicized activity with which they should have no truck. In particular, if a corporation enjoys market dominance because of internal growth, it should not be penalized by the courts; business efficiency and the success it brings should not be confused with artificial barriers to entry and unfair competitive advantage. Designed to prevent big business from using its muscle to the detriment of consumers, what anti-trust legislation all too often succeeds in doing, according to Bork, is giving protection and subsidies to inefficient small businesses; this is part of the paradox that Bork refers to in his title. He goes on to argue that debates about anti-trust cases are a microcosm of the struggle to preserve liberal capitalist societies against their anti-market, egalitarian enemies.

A sophisticated defence of monopoly is put forward in the work of two American economists, Stanley Liebowitz and Stephen Margolis. Examining the evidence in a number of notorious cases of ostensible market failure, they argue that the facts do not support the case for the prosecution. A spectacular example concerns the action brought by the US Department of Justice against Microsoft. Liebowitz and Margolis (2001) argue that Microsoft's market dominance in word-processing and spreadsheet applications is due not to abuses of monopoly power but to the superiority of the company's software. Microsoft enjoys a deserved near-monopoly in these applications. Its success is also due to competitive pricing: Microsoft's entry into software markets caused prices to decline rapidly, and when Microsoft achieved market dominance, prices continued to fall.

'Serial monopoly', where firms compete to control the whole market, is characteristic of new information technology. Computer software is a paradigm case. In 1986, WordPerfect was the market leader in word processing, with a little under 20 per cent market share, closely followed by WordStar, the former leader. By 1990, WordPerfect had established itself in clear first place, with just under 50 per cent market share. It was popular with corporations, software reviewers and individual users. Yet only six years later, WordPerfect had been blown away while Microsoft Word for Windows had captured almost 90 per cent of the market.

The reasons for this transformation were not, if Liebowitz and Stephen Margolis are to be believed, mysterious. Until the 1990s, personal computers were based on MS-DOS, a disk operating system which required users to memorize a set of keyboard commands just as if they were scientists or mathematicians performing calculations on a mainframe computer. The introduction of Windows has changed all that; people simply use a mouse to click on windows, icons and menus, with no need to remember commands or consult weighty manuals. As MS-DOS gave way to Windows, a new wave of competition swept through the industry. The WordPerfect Corporation was slow to respond, and its early versions of WordPerfect for Windows were inferior to Microsoft's Word, as software reviews clearly attest. Microsoft also had an excellent spreadsheet programme, Excel, which it was able to incorporate with Word in its Office suite, making it particularly attractive to corporate clients.

The critical point in Liebowitz and Margolis's analysis is that Microsoft has learned the basic lesson of serial monopoly. Even when it has a dominant market share, it still worries about *potential* competitors. It has seen, from the collapse of the market for WordPerfect, that behaving like a textbook monopolist – raising prices to exploit a stranglehold on the market, or failing to innovate because there are no serious competitors – does not succeed in the fast-moving world of information technology. Its alertness to actual and potential competitors, not its monopoly, explains why, having gained leadership in a particular market, Microsoft has never lost it.

For Liebowitz and Margolis, the Microsoft case is the latest in a series of urban myths about market failure. Other famous cases include the QWERTY typewriter keyboard, and the victory of the VHS video-tape format over Beta.

According to the urban myth, the QWERTY layout, patented in 1868, was deliberately designed to prevent secretaries from typing so fast that the hammers jammed. More efficient keyboard layouts have been designed, but none of them have succeeded. QWERTY established an early lead and no other layout could compete; for well over a century, hundreds of millions of people have been using an inferior design – surely a perverse failure of the market?

As for VHS video tape, the urban myth is that the Beta format was technically superior. VHS's victory was due to slick marketing; it rapidly achieved market dominance largely because retail and rental outlets stocked it. People chose VHS because it was the market leader. They wanted a wide choice of films to hire or buy, and to exchange tapes with their friends. As with the QWERTY keyboard, consumers were locked into an inferior technology because everybody else was.

In both these cases, Liebowitz and Margolis find no evidence to support the myths. QWERTY is not an inferior technology; no methodologically valid experiments have been conducted to demonstrate that QWERTY is significantly outperformed by any rival. Beta was not superior to VHS; software reviews at the time of their development showed that there was little to choose between them. Beta actually came to market first, which ought to have given it an advantage. The crucial point, overlooked by the myth, is that the Sony corporation designed Beta to be small and relatively portable, whereas Matsushita designed VHS to have a long playing time. Matsushita was right and Sony was wrong; people were more interested in playing time than portability, which is why VHS came from behind to overtake Beta. The market did not fail, it succeeded.

These cases raise serious doubts about market failure. They suggest that consumers rarely, if ever, get 'locked into' inferior technologies owing to the accidents of history. The core reason for this lies in the market mechanism. The market is a place where profit-maximizing entrepreneurs and utility-maximizing consumers seek one another out. Entrepreneurs want to develop better mousetraps, consumers want to purchase them, and intermediaries want to bring them together. Only in a command economy will this fail to happen.

Liebowitz and Margolis's work can be read as a counterblast to left-wing thinking on the market. Leftist intellectuals may find it hard to accept that progress is made not by implementing their own blueprints for the good society, but by leaving it to mutual adjustments among entrepreneurs and consumers. Liebowitz and Margolis are also critical of fellow economists for their apparent lack of faith in real-life markets. As we saw above, the market, or at least the perfectly competitive market, has become an abstract theoretical state shorn, paradoxically, of competitiveness. In celebrating the market system, Liebowitz and Margolis point us towards the social reality of markets. In that sense, if in no other, they stand in the 'Austrian' tradition of economics alongside Hayek, whose work was discussed in chapter 1.

The market according to Liebowitz and Margolis is, just as for Hayek, an arena where entrepreneurs and consumers interact to their mutual profit. Interestingly, this treats the modern corporation as simply an entrepreneur whose goods and services are purchased by consumers. It ignores the fact that many of us relate to corporations not just as consumers but also as employees. I am using Microsoft Word to prepare the text of this book. From my perspective, the reason is straightforward, and it is not the one given by Liebowitz and Margolis. I have not selected Word because I have independently evaluated it as the best word-processing programme on the market. On a purely personal note, I find many of its features irritating; I preferred WordPerfect. I have chosen Word simply because my university, in keeping with most others, selected it as the standard software for university use and purchased a site licence from Microsoft. For all official communications within and on behalf of the university, I am instructed to use Word; I am even told which font to use (this promotes the university's corporate identity). Given these requirements, the costs to me of adopting another package are too high. My university in effect obliged me to abandon WordPerfect. The university, itself a corporation, has acted as my agent; it has chosen for me. Liebowitz and Margolis may like to assume that the corporation's interests and my own are identical. I invite readers to consider whether such a proposition is true of their own lives.

Market-based Solutions: Protecting the Environment

Is the capitalist free market compatible with conserving the environment for the enjoyment of future generations? Can capitalism be green?

The obvious answer would appear to be 'no'. Environmental degradation presents itself as an inevitable consequence of capitalism's pursuit of profit. The solution surely must be dramatic political interventions to protect the planet against the ravages of the unrestrained free market.

Following Saunders's lead (1995: 52–76), we may distinguish three approaches to the problem of using the market to generate solutions beneficial to the environment. The first of these is to harness the power of green consumerism. If there is a demand for environmentally friendly products, entrepreneurs will compete to supply them. The late twentieth century saw a large number of profitable ventures in green consumerism, including fairly traded tea and coffee, environmentally friendly detergents, cosmetics free from testing on animals, organic and biodynamic produce, biodegradable packaging, recycling programmes for household waste, furniture from sustainable developments, ethical and environmental investments, fuel-efficient engines, low-emission fuels, renewable energy sources, and, in the case of products lacking these qualities, consumer boycotts. Green consumer organizations aim to raise consciousness about the environment and disseminate objective information about green products.

Green consumerism is clearly compatible with the free market; the problem is its limitations. Green products have established a market niche, certainly, but they come at a premium price, one which not all consumers will wish to pay. Corporations parade the green credentials of their products, but there may be an element of sham in this; 'free range eggs' conjure up the image of chickens wandering around an idyllic farmyard, but this picture may be false, and consumers may find it hard to know where the truth lies. Green consumerism may be a very light shade of green, as shown by the market for 'environmental' investment funds, some of which invest on a 'best of the bunch' principle, choosing, for example, the oil company that does least damage to the environment. Finally, green consumption tends to be just that: consumption. Fairly traded coffee is not marketed on the principle that we should drink less of it. If a commitment to the environment means rejecting the 'growth fetish' (Hamilton, C. 2004) and consuming less, green consumerism cannot be the answer.

The second market-based approach is for governments to use the price system to encourage environmentally friendly activities. They may, for instance, introduce charges on access to resources which hitherto had been subsidized or free at the point of use. Tolls on motorways and bridges, and congestion charges in cities, are an effective way of reducing traffic congestion, since they encourage consumers who do not wish to pay the charge to find alternative routes, use public transport, form a car pool, cycle, walk or simply stay away.

As an example of this second approach, Saunders cites the policy of reducing the tax on unleaded petrol, as many West European countries did in the 1980s. Very rapidly, most consumers switched from leaded fuel, and car manufacturers ceased to produce cars requiring it. No regulation and no bureaucracy: self-interested consumers and manufacturers brought about the desired social change rapidly and efficiently, thanks to the price mechanism. A few motorists continued to drive old-fashioned cars requiring expensive leaded petrol; but, from a market perspective, so what? At least the polluter was paying. An additional solution has now been developed by the market: lead replacement petrol, which has the same engineering properties but without the lead.

The third market-based approach to environmental protection is to create, where possible, property rights in public goods. Currently the most controversial technique is the use of tradable pollution permits. The relevant authority – the government, or an international agency – decides how much pollution to permit. Every firm (or country) has the right to pollute up to the limit, but are charged if they exceed it. The key innovation here is to make these rights to pollute tradable. Firms that can economically reduce their pollution will sell their right to pollute to firms that find it more expensive to do so. Tradable rights to pollute mean that the least cost, most efficient solution will be found to reaching desired overall reduction in pollution: firm A will reduce its pollution, and this will be paid for by firm B, which continues to pollute but pays the price. Both firms will be better off than if they had been required to cut pollution equally. Overall, the target reduction in pollution will be achieved, but by a more efficient route than if all firms were required to reduce their pollution to the target level. It is, perhaps, an acid test of one's attitude towards the market to decide whether or not this is a convincing solution to the problem of pollution.

Is and Ought: The Market as Ideology

Each of the three pro-market ideologies examined in this chapter highlights a different set of the benefits of the market as set out in table 1.1 (see p. 31). Market populism emphasizes *choice, consumer sovereignty* and *freedom*: markets are truly democratic. The Efficient Market Hypothesis affirms the *dynamism* of markets and the *prosperity* that flows from it: markets are more efficient than any other system of production, distribution and exchange. Market fundamentalism emphasizes *prosperity* and *freedom*: the market is the good society in action, it has triumphed over its enemies, and 'the end of history' is at hand.

How, then, do these pro-market ideologies address the challenges to the market that are listed in the second column of table 1.1? *Commodity fetishism, dehumanization* and *hegemony* are dismissed as the obsessions of intellectuals who resent the limited role the market gives them, and attempt to protect their stock of cultural capital by denigrating the products of the market and the people who consume them. *Corporate power* is not simply accepted as a necessary element of advanced market systems, but also pronounced to be the servant of the will of the people. Finally, *inequality* is justified as the outcome of choice, the corollary of prosperity and the price of freedom.

A striking feature of pro-market ideologies is their treatment of market failure. Despite acknowledging that market failure is conceivable, they regard it as a rare occurrence caused by *external* factors – imperfections, typically the result of government interference – that disrupt the free operation of the market. Market failure is, moreover, defined in a special way: it occurs when a market falls short of 'economic efficiency' as conceived by neoclassical economics.

Neoclassical economics operates with a set of logically interconnected concepts, such as economic efficiency, Pareto optimum, perfect competition, market imperfections and market failure. Together they form a deductive system that is highly coherent and resistant to critique. It poses a characteristic question: are you for us or against us?

Many of the central terms used to analyse the market are strikingly value-loaded: economic *efficiency*, Pareto *optimum*, *perfect* competition, *normal* goods, market *imperfections*, market *failure*. Is it reasonable, or ethical, to be against an optimum and in favour of failure? An approach that claims to be value-free is shot through with evaluative terms, blurring the distinction between analysis and prescription. To explain this contradiction we can draw on the work of Mary Douglas (1966), interpreting the market anthropologically as an expression of beliefs about purity and danger. The market represents purity, in the sense of social order and social cohesion. It is threatened by pollution, that is by forces of ambiguity, disruption and disorder. Purity and danger, order and chaos: the veneer of rationality in theories of the market fails to suppress an emotionally charged symbolism.

As thinking about the market evolved, a movement toward abstraction became dominant. This can be illustrated through the concept of perfect competition. To Adam Smith and his contemporaries, as Backhouse (2002: 327) points out, 'competition was a process: people competed with each other in the same way that horses competed on the racecourse'. Competition meant effort and rivalry, as it does to most people. This is precisely what is lacking in the situation known to economists as perfect competition, a theoretical state in which resource allocation is optimal and market power absent. Under perfect competition, each firm is so small relative to the overall market that it cannot affect prices; it simply has to 'take' the prices that are set by the forces of supply and demand. Ironically, firms in a perfectly competitive market have no incentive to behave competitively.

Literature on the market displays a recurrent slippage between three things: describing how markets actually operate, generating abstract analytic models, and prescribing how social exchanges should ideally take place. The slippage is between *is*, *as if*, and *ought*. In the economic literature, analysis is prioritized, prescription is politically imperative even though it is often denied, while description of actual markets comes a poor third. Yet the plausibility of analysis and prescription trades off our experience of social interactions in a variety of marketplaces. Markets can, admittedly, be dangerous and risky, so let the buyer beware. Let the seller beware, too: the murky canvas found in an attic might just be a Bruegel. Despite these risks, or rather because of them, markets connote freedom, autonomy, choice, innovation, richness, colour, character, identity, tradition and heritage. They stand in bright contrast to bureaucracy and hierarchy. The appeal of *the market* as theoretical construct and political programme depends, illicitly, on our experiences of the social reality of *markets*.

3
The Social Reality of Markets

The market system – both as a complex of social institutions and practices, and as a set of concepts and theories that construct the market as an object of enquiry and an analytic tool – provides an answer to a core sociological question: how is social order possible? It is a paradoxical answer, depicting social co-ordination that lacks a co-ordinator and that is achieved less by consciously planned endeavour than through the unintended consequences of a myriad of human actions.

As we have seen, this potentially rich idea of the market can all too easily become impoverished. Co-ordination can be seen as somehow 'automatic', as if it were a naturally occurring event. Human agency is reduced to calculation of material advantage. Culture becomes a 'dimension' of social life, amounting to little more than a sporadically invoked device to shore up a theory whenever it faces an unanswerable challenge. The aim of this chapter is to examine sociological work which offers, following Callon's warning (1998: 50), 'not a more complex *homo economicus* but the comprehension of his simplicity and poverty'. This work aims to restore the human to human agency, the social to social order and the cultural to cultural life.

The Problem of Social Order

The theory of co-ordination by mutual adjustment was powerfully restated in the nineteenth century in the prolific writings of Herbert Spencer. Like Adam Smith before him, Spencer believed that industrial societies are not held together by shared beliefs or by state regulation. On the contrary, social equilibrium would be jeopardized by conformity to moral consensus or the authority of the state. What he called 'militant' societies, which were based on 'compulsory co-ordination', could not survive the evolutionary struggle with industrial societies. As societies evolved from the militant to the industrial type, so regulation declined, particularly in economic life; Spencer was a firm advocate of laissez-faire. For him, as for Smith, industrial society is a system whose coherence is guaranteed by innumerable acts of mutual accommodation that occur through the processes of bargaining and social exchange.

In his first great work, *The Division of Labour in Society* (1984/1897), Émile Durkheim contested Spencer's theory. He argued that social solidarity could not be based on the free play of individual interests. Such a market could not produce harmony but only provisional and tactical truces; conflict would always be latent and in that sense merely deferred. Nor was Spencer's account of social evolution accurate. Far from having declined, social regulation of individuals was greater in industrial societies than in earlier, simpler types. Industrial society was more complex and differentiated, and therefore needed a more fine-grained system of laws.

Durkheim famously argued that Spencer had overlooked 'the non-contractual element in the contract'. Contracts may be made between individuals, but it is society which gives them their force. Spencer's analysis is the wrong way round; as Slater and Tonkiss put it (2001: 83): 'Neither market exchange nor social order results from individuals entering into contracts; rather, individuals, contracts and exchanges make sense only against the background of a social order.' Without the moral authority of society, internalized as norms and values and sanctioned by mechanisms of social control, market exchanges would rapidly degenerate into chaos.

As Durkheim's career unfolded, it became ever clearer that he was totally at odds with the brand of individualism associated with Spencer and the economists (Lukes 1973). Their individualism was narrowly utilitarian, commercial and materialistic. It celebrated the cult of the self, painting a sad portrait of human beings as isolated egoists. Durkheim too was committed to individualism, but of a very different variety. The individualism he championed was morally charged and outward-looking; it affirmed respect for human rights, the dignity of the individual and the universal demands of justice. In a strong sense of word, individualism was the *sacred* principle on which the social cohesion of industrial society depended. It was, he contended, a secular consequence of Christian values.

Early on in *The Structure of Social Action*, Parsons (1937) similarly emphasized that individualism is deeply rooted in Western culture. It is a core value of Christianity, reinforced after the Protestant Reformation and given a further twist by secularization. A thoroughly undesirable result has been that social theorists, incorporating an excessively individualist approach into their own work, have neglected the processes by which the goals of human action are integrated into stable social systems.

Economics, Parsons argues, is based on atomistic individualism, and therefore cannot give a satisfactory answer to the question: 'how does society hold together?' Individuals, according to atomistic individualism, pursue ends that they have freely chosen, ends which the economist treats as given. What guarantee is there, then, that people's goals will be compatible? Why will the outcome not be what the seventeenth-century political philosopher Thomas Hobbes called a war of all against all?

Parsons highlighted four features of what he called the 'utilitarian' social theory embodied in economics: *atomism* – a tendency to focus on individual acts isolated from a social or cultural context; *rationality* – emphasizing instrumental rationality, the rationality or efficiency of means, rather than ends that are valued in themselves; *empiricism* – seeing social systems simply as aggregates of individual actions; and *randomness of ends* – ignoring ways in which the ends of action do or do not harmonize with one another, and treating the outcomes of individual actions as pure chance.

Parsons' crucial point is that utilitarian theory fails to give an adequate explanation of social order. On a utilitarian account, society will be characterized by unbridled struggles for power. As Hobbes saw, people will have no reason not to use force and fraud to serve their own ends. To prevent a war of all against all, he argued, power would have to be vested in a sovereign who would coerce obedience.

Reacting against his predecessor's authoritarian solution to the problem of social order, John Locke postulated a 'natural harmony of interests' between people. His almost mystical appeal to benign human nature may be attractive, but it has no justification within utilitarian theory; according to Parsons, it is an illegitimate move designed to prop up a fatally flawed approach.

Parsons' own solution to the problem of order was to reject all forms of utilitarian theory in favour of a 'voluntaristic' theory of action, one which emphasizes the function of shared social values that orient action towards common goals. Social interaction is governed by culturally transmitted norms and values which regulate and render predictable the behaviour of others. The process of socialization, above all in the family and at school, ensures that individuals internalize these norms and values. A shared value system is, for Parsons, the bedrock of social order.

Nineteen years later, Parsons made his second major contribution to the sociological understanding of the market. *Economy and Society*, co-authored with Neil Smelser, is subtitled 'a study in the integration of economic and social theory'. Parsons and Smelser announce in the preface that the book is designed as a contribution to the synthesis of theory in economics and sociology. They speak of the intrinsic intimacy between the two sister disciplines, and call for a rapprochement between them. The intellectual barriers between the two are largely a product of mutual misunderstanding, aggravated by the fact that few theorists are well versed in both.

A distinctive departure from Parsons' earlier work is the claim that economic theory treats 'the economy' as a sub-system differentiated from other sub-systems of a society. Drawing on his theory of four 'functional imperatives' which any society has to address, he and Smelser argue that the economy is principally concerned with the function of adaptation. The four sub-systems and their functions are as follows:

- *The adaptation sub-system* (A)   The goal of the economy is to produce wealth, which Parsons and Smelser treat as a generalized capacity to command goods and services.
- *The goal-attainment sub-system* (G)   If the adaptation sub-system is in effect the economy, then the goal-attainment sub-system is the polity. The function of the polity is to mobilize a society's resources, including its wealth, in pursuit of collective goals.
- *The integrative sub-system* (I)   This function of this sub-system is social control through a system of legal and social norms governing individual behaviour. The integrative sub-system controls deviance and promotes conditions favouring social harmony.
- *The latent pattern-maintenance sub-system* (L)   This sub-system is a society's culture, its institutionalized value-system into which individuals are socialized, and which gives them motivation and a sense of identity.

A key point for Parsons and Smelser is that each of these four sub-systems has its own internal sub-system made up of A, G, I and L. Their analysis of the economy focuses both on its interactions with the polity, the system of social control, and the value-system, and also on the exchanges within the economy between its own A, G, I and L functions.

Parsons' contributions have not been well regarded by later generations. To be informed that 'economic theory is a special case of the general theory of social systems' was never likely to commend itself to economists, implying as it does the socio-logical colonization of economics. And since Parsons and Smelser's work contains nothing recognizable as a formula, rejects mathematization, and offers no concrete predictions, most economists would see no advantage in embracing the Parsonian paradigm.

In *The Structure of Social Action* (1937), Parsons had refused to criticize economics for making artificial simplify-ing assumptions about 'economic man'. All social scientific theory has an irreducibly abstract quality; to criticize it on that ground, demanding that it be more 'realistic', is to commit the fallacy of 'misplaced concreteness'. Instead, Parsons proposed a controversial division of labour between sociology and economics. The task economics quite properly sets itself is to analyse the chain connecting means to ends in a situation of scarce resources; the ends of human endeavour are taken as given. Sociology, in contrast, focuses on the values which shape and give meaning to human action, and the norms which guide it. On one reading (for example, Slater and Tonkiss 2001: 23), Parsons was happy to see economics and sociology as disciplines that complemented each other. His compromise failed, however, to satisfy either party. Most sociologists think that he made too many concessions to economics, while economists, if they pay any attention to his proposals, tend to see them as an attack on the market.

Holton (1992) is one of the few commentators on the sociology of economic life who sees significant merit in the Parsonian paradigm. According to him, *Economy and Society* has three great strengths as a contribution to sociological theorizing on economic life. It avoids reductionism, offering a multidimensional theory of economy and society; it combines an examination of the internal workings of the economy with an analysis of the interactions between economy and society; and it takes into account both constraints and opportunities. The programme, for Holton, amounts to a radical approach that rejects both the bland faith of liberals in market solutions, and the pessimism of political economic approaches that emphasize the coercive operation of power and the endemic conflicts of interest in the market system (Holton 1992: 267–8).

Despite Holton's defence, recent work by sociologists has remained lukewarm about Parsons' contribution to the sociology of economic life. Fevre's *The New Sociology of Economic Behaviour* (2003) contains two passing references to Parsons; Fligstein's *The Architecture of Markets* (2001) has none. Smart's *Economy, Culture and Society* (2003) has a brief summary of Parsons' contribution, echoing the familiar criticisms. Slater and Tonkiss (2001) offer a two-page account of his work, in which they agree with Wrong's judgement that Parsons had an 'over-socialized' concept of humanity (Wrong 1961), and conclude that Parsons fails to provide an adequate account of the cultural dimension of economic action. Perhaps most tellingly of all, du Gay and Pryke's edited collection, *Cultural Economy* (2002), contains eleven papers, not one of which makes any reference at all to Parsons or Smelser.

Three elements in such adverse reactions to Parsons deserve to be questioned. First, while it is true that he did provide some support to neoclassical economic orthodoxy in its conflict with so-called institutional economics, this was scarcely to endorse the neoclassical paradigm. What Parsons was defending was not neoclassical economics but social theorizing, which is necessarily abstract. For Parsons, the defence of theory had paramount importance. This is shown graphically by his comparison of Hobbes and Locke. Hobbes's analysis of the problem of order was flawed. His 'iron consistency' in developing utilitarian theory may have led him to empirical errors, such as an excessive fear of social revolution, but his was nevertheless 'a greater scientific achievement than Locke's more "reasonable" attitude', which failed adequately to separate out his implicit normative assumptions from established fact. Locke 'was right but gave the wrong reasons' (Parsons 1937: 97n). Although closer to the truth, Locke was the less penetrating and productive thinker. The key thing is that Hobbes was paid a greater compliment than Locke – but Hobbes was wrong even so. That is exactly Parsons' view of neoclassical economic theory.

It follows, second, that Parsons' view of economics is not so approving as it has been made to appear. The idea that his sociology made too many concessions to economics is, significantly, not a view that economists share.

Third, we have already seen the criticism, voiced by Slater and Tonkiss, that Parsons provides an inadequate account of the cultural dimension of economic action. It may be so; though his emphasis on culturally transmitted norms and values, and his and Smelser's insistence that the economy has its own latent pattern maintenance sub system, that is to say its own culture, scarcely suggest that culture is added as a kind of afterthought, a mere 'dimension' of economic activity (Slater and Tonkiss 2001: 90). Such a view does little justice to Parsons' trenchant critique of the theory that social order is produced by the mutual adjustment of atomistic individuals.

A Question of Trust

There is a strong case for saying that trust is an essential ingredient of the human condition. Arguably all social theory incorporates tacit assumptions about trust; in some theoretical work the issue is made explicit. Harold Garfinkel's ethnomethodology provides an outstanding example.

Garfinkel shared Parsons' focus on the problem of social order, a problem at the core of Durkheimian sociology (Garfinkel 2002). Parsons emphasized that social order depends upon institutionalized values and norms, a common culture into which people are socialized. According to Garfinkel this takes too much for granted, and does not penetrate to the heart of the problem. People must be able to view the world in the same terms, they must agree on the meanings of actions, before they can co-ordinate their activities. The cognitive problem of order is fundamental (Heritage 1984: 305). Social life is a collaborative enterprise in which we come to understand one another by using our experience and imagination to interpret the meaning of what people say and do. We rely implicitly on one another's capacities and preparedness to construct and maintain this shared universe. Social order is, then, a practical achievement of skilful agents, 'ordinary' people using 'everyday' methodologies – ethnomethodologies – to make sense of the world. We are not 'cultural dopes' constrained by our socialization into norms and values, but active agents who achieve social order through ongoing social interactions in which we report and account for our actions, thereby demonstrating their meaning to ourselves and others.

For Garfinkel, this collaborative work of fashioning shared meanings is a moral as well as a cognitive requirement – it is a question of trust. His 'breaching experiments' (Garfinkel 1967), in which researchers deliberately violated the norms governing interactions in particular settings, rapidly provoked bewilderment and anger, thereby revealing the amount of cultural energy locked up in everyday taken-for-granted interactions which appear, but are not, banal and unproblematic. Given this, as Heritage remarks (1984: 309), social conformity is shown to be not an unreflecting product of the prior internalization of norms, but as contingent upon people's awareness of how deviant actions will be interpreted. Conformity, as we may be more or less consciously aware, is not incompatible with self-interest. Perhaps, then, although he does not make the point himself, Garfinkel's ethnomethodological programme, defined at the outset as the study of the methods used by people to produce meaningful social order, bears some similarity to Adam's Smith view of the market as co-ordination by mutual adjustment, made possible by humanity's propensity 'to truck, barter, and exchange one thing with another'.

Anthony Giddens (1991) also addresses trust directly, drawing on Garfinkel but also on Erikson's ego-psychology. For Erikson, in the first stage of human development a properly socialized infant learns to place a basic trust in the world, owing to its experience of nursing, feeding and the warm physical presence of caring adults, particularly the mother. Such infants recognize goodness in themselves and others. They enjoy ontological security: an assured sense of their own identity, and a conviction that there is order in the world, in people and events. Infants who do not receive such care will develop a basic mistrust, a pathological state involving anxiety and fear of malevolence from others. Trust is a necessary risk and involves a leap of faith, in that we place our confidence in other people despite a lack of full information. The crucial problem in the modern world is not that we lack full information – this has always been so – but that we are forced to trust not only people but abstract impersonal systems managed by corporations and bureaucracies. Such systems depend on trust, yet they provide none of the moral rewards which can be obtained from trust vested in people (Giddens 1991: 136). Trust loses some of its moral quality and becomes more pragmatic and calculative.

If Garfinkel's microsociological analysis demonstrates that trust is a universal property of social interaction, Giddens's comments point towards a specifically modern dilemma in the dynamics of trust. The problem was expressed concisely by Georg Simmel in an essay published in 1908. 'Our modern life', he wrote, 'is based to a much larger extent than is usually realized upon the faith in the honesty of the other. Examples are our economy, which becomes more and more a credit economy, or our science, in which most scholars must use innumerable results of other scientists which they cannot examine. We base our gravest decisions on a complex system of conceptions most of which presuppose the confidence that we will not be betrayed' (Simmel 1950/1908: 313).

Simmel's analysis underscores the problem of trust in modern urban societies, where relationships are typically impersonal. On what basis should we trust a stranger? Conversely, how can we convince strangers that we are trustworthy ourselves? How can we overcome the gross asymmetry of a situation where the stranger probably knows whether or not he is lying, while we cannot tell? As we saw in chapter 2, information asymmetry is one cause of serious market failure. 'Let the buyer beware' is a prudent warning against foolishness; but basic mistrust cannot be the foundation of psychic health or social order.

Max Weber addressed this problem in his paper, 'The Protestant sects and the spirit of capitalism' (Weber 1948/ 1923), which he wrote as a kind of afterword to his classic work on the Protestant ethic. If the United States in the early twentieth century was a society of mass immigration, rapid urban growth and extensive social and geographical mobility, how could trust be established in social interactions? Weber's answer was to point to the social significance of religious commitment. People with a strong religious faith had good reasons to trust people with similar convictions. In the case of strict Protestant communities, 'Admission to the congregation is recognized as an absolute guarantee of the moral qualities of a gentleman, especially of those qualities required in business matters. It is crucial that sect membership meant a certificate of moral qualification and especially of business morals for the individual' (Weber 1948/1923: 305). Sects not only had strict entry requirements; they also imposed continuing high standards of conduct on their members, and were prepared to expel anyone who failed to live up to their demands. Sect membership therefore provided a good warrant of moral rectitude and trustworthiness. No wonder, Weber observed, that in the United States the question of a person's religious affiliation was so prominent in business dealings.

The implication of Weber's analysis, in keeping with his cultural pessimism, is not reassuring. His point is that the American society of his own day was not 'a formless sand heap of individuals, but rather a buzzing complex of strictly exclusive, yet voluntary associations' (Weber 1948/1923: 310). A person's character was vouched for by his or her active participation in self-policing voluntary associations with high moral principles. This world, says Weber, is decaying; society is becoming more atomized. Weber's analysis is not a solution to Simmel's dilemma of modernity but a confirmation of it.

If caveat emptor, let the buyer beware, is the watchword of the market, credat emptor, let the buyer believe, is often said to be the principle that should govern the relationship between professionals and their clients. Surprisingly, this appears to have been Adam Smith's view, despite his opposition to all forms of combination in restraint of trade as conspiracies against the public. What keeps any occupation up to the mark, according to him, is not governance by a guild or professional association, but market forces: 'The pretence that corporations are necessary for the better government of the trade, is without any foundation. The real and effectual discipline which is exercised over a workman, is not that of his corporation, but that of his customers' (Smith 1976/1776: 146). Provided there is no restraint on competition, consumers have the ultimate weapon: taking their custom elsewhere. Fear of going out of business, not fear of a professional body, is what ensures good professional service.

And yet Smith also wrote this: 'We trust our health to the physician; our fortune and sometimes our life and reputation to the lawyer and attorney. Such confidence could not safely be reposed in people of a very mean or low condition. Their reward must be such, therefore, as may give them that rank in the society which so important a trust requires' (Smith 1976/1776: 122). How can we account for the blatant contradiction between his rejection of combinations and his endorsement of the self-advancing actions of professional associations?

Dingwall and Fenn (1987) offer a subtle explanation of the paradox. Professional associations stand for high ideals of professionalism embodied in professional ethics and codes of practice. The pre-industrial concept of 'honour' is a live force among professionals. We know that this is so, and recognize the humiliation faced by professionals who are publicly disgraced. Given such a powerful sanction, and given that most professionals are sincere in their commitment, our confidence in the professions is not blind faith but rationally grounded (Dingwall 1999: 133). As Simmel saw, information is inevitably distributed unequally between professionals and their clients. Professional associations inspire public confidence not only in the professions themselves but in this inescapable asymmetry of market society. Far from constituting a failure of the market, professional bodies exist in order to redress a potential market failure – a failure of trust.

The tensions in Smith's approach to the professions are reflected in a remarkable recantation made by Eliot Freidson. His *Profession of Medicine*, first published in 1970, concluded with two trenchant chapters entitled 'The Limits of Professional Knowledge' and 'The Limits of Professional Autonomy'. He argues that privilege and power, not expertise, is what distinguishes many 'experts'; that much that is paraded as expertise is merely a concealed class morality that seeks to discipline the lower orders; and that professionals tend to impose their own norms and values on clients whom they judge to be ignorant and irrational. Expertise is 'more and more in danger of being used as a mask for privilege and power rather than, as it claims, as a mode of advancing the public interest' (Freidson 1975: 337).

As for professional ethics, while ethical *intent* may or may not be sincere, it too seldom informs actual *performance*. Blinded by the glitter of their own status, professions are in danger of mistaking rhetoric for reality. Freidson warns (1975: 381) of the real threat of 'a new tyranny which sincerely expresses itself in the language of humanitarianism and which imposes its own values on others for what it sees to be their own good'. In sheltering professionals from serious scrutiny, professional autonomy poses a major challenge to a free society. His robust conclusion (1975: 382) is a call to strip away professional privilege and cant, since 'the professions' role in a free society should be limited to contributing the technical information men need to make their own decisions on the basis of their own values'.

By the time he came to write his *Professionalism: the third logic* (2001), Freidson had renounced his earlier critique. Instead of emphasizing their technical expertise, he mounts a staunch defence of the social value of professions, placing particular weight on professional ethics.

He begins by emphasizing the inescapable inequality of knowledge and expertise between professionals and their clients. Neither organized consumerism, nor improved education, nor wider access to databases of information, can overcome this gulf. To believe otherwise is to fall victim to the chimera of 'populist generalism' – the refusal to recognize that the sheer quantity, complexity and opacity of specialized knowledge make it impossible for lay people to be empowered to make rational choices without professional advice. With its claim to challenge professional privilege and elitism, populist generalism has an obvious affinity with countercultural radical thought. What Freidson also stresses is the support populist generalism receives from the ideology of the free market, in which the consumer is sovereign. From the perspective of free marketeers, social closure and monopoly enable professions to extract excessive profits from their clients by abusing market power.

For Freidson, the key to rebutting populist generalism is to rekindle faith in professional associations as the guardians of professional ethics. Professional bodies must enjoy a high degree of independence from the state and the market. The contemporary travails of professionalism are caused by a crisis that is not economic or structural, but cultural. What is at stake is professionalism's 'soul'. If professional codes of ethics are to carry any conviction with the public, they must be vigorously enforced by professional institutions that pursue violations relentlessly, thereby preserving the profession's good name and validating the true professionalism of the vast majority of practitioners. The crisis of trust in professions is caused by the ideology of the free market; professionalism must reassert itself as an anti-market value-system if market failure is to be averted.

Contemporary societies require their citizens to place trust not only in persons but in abstract systems. This is more problematic and less rewarding psychologically than vesting trust in personal relationships, yet it is essential to the functioning of the modern world. Fukuyama (1995: 4) argues that 'a nation's well-being, as well as its ability to compete, is conditioned by a single, pervasive cultural characteristic: the level of trust inherent in the society'. The wealth of nations is made up not just of economic capital but of social and cultural capital. Borrowing Coleman's understanding of social capital as people's ability to work together for common purposes in groups and organizations, Fukuyama argues that the stock of social capital is dwindling, as community declines and individuals clamour for their rights. Law, contract and economic rationality: these features of the market are necessary but not sufficient for social order and prosperity, and must be supplemented by the non-market forces of reciprocity, moral obligation, duty and trust.

Embeddedness, Trust – and Fraud

Accepting the validity of Parsons' critique of atomistic individualism, many sociologists argue that his own theory went too far to the opposite pole, placing undue emphasis on value consensus and painting a portrait of actors almost wholly constrained by the socialization process through which they have internalized those values. An atomized economic man freely choosing his own goals has been traded for an 'over-socialized' actor who has little freedom of choice, but who 'acts' as a vehicle of his or her society's culture. What is missing, the critics say, is a focus on the multiple ways in which culture is actively negotiated and constructed through social interaction.

Among sociologists seeking a middle way between the extremes, an influential contribution was made by Mark Granovetter in his widely cited paper, 'Economic action and social structure: the problem of embeddedness' (1985). He argues that Parsonian theory, for all its emphasis on cultural values, paradoxically replicates a quality of economic utilitarian theory that it seeks to repudiate: an atomistic view of the human actor. Economic man pursues his self-interest unconstrained by culture; over-socialized man enacts internalized norms and values *without being significantly influenced by ongoing social relations*.

Granovetter's concerns are neatly illustrated by the problem of trust, discussed above. He points out that most economic theory, despite its concept of economic rationality, tacitly assumes that one's economic interest is pursued only by comparatively gentlemanly means (1985: 488). This is the error that Parsons found in Locke: an unwarranted assumption that most people will 'naturally' behave in a civilized manner, as though civilization were not a product of society. Hobbes was correct in seeing that nothing in the concept of the rational pursuit of self-interest prevents the use of force or fraud. Why not take advantage of them, if they are effective and efficient? According to Granovetter, Hobbes's clear perception of the implications of atomistic individualism was watered down by Adam Smith, who portrays the pursuit of economic self-interest as a civilized activity – thereby assuming what has to be proved. Smith's atomized actors turn out to be nothing of the sort; inexplicably, they have internalized norms and values of fair trading that preclude force and fraud.

Some economists, consistent with atomistic individualism, argue that regulatory institutions have evolved so as to discourage fraud by making it too costly. The crucial problem with this solution, Granovetter says, is that it does not involve trust but relies in Hobbesian fashion on sovereign authorities that police behaviour and punish wrongdoing. Since they are based not on trust but on disincentives to wrongdoing, such institutional arrangements cannot restrain clever people from seeking ways to evade detection and punishment. Economic life would, on this logic, be 'poisoned by ever more ingenious attempts at deceit' (Granovetter 1985: 489).

A few economists, anxious to take 'social institutions' and 'culture' into account, point to trust as part of society's value-system, a generalized morality that requires us all to behave honestly. Up to a point, this carries conviction. If every social encounter were underpinned by profound mistrust, social order would be impossible. The problem with this approach is that, like Parsons' theory, it takes an oversocialized view of human action. It places too much weight on generalized trust, and incorrectly implies that society is a community of saints. Basic mistrust may be pathological; but if we acted on the naïve assumption that everyone we deal with is totally honest in every respect, we should be easy targets for any confidence trickster. We might also find ourselves not praised for being trusting but blamed for being foolish. The law might not offer compensation if we were judged to have acted irresponsibly.

Granovetter's own approach focuses on the embeddedness of action in social networks. He points to the widespread preference for dealing with people and institutions that enjoy a high reputation; in our everyday life, we hesitate to rely simply on regulatory institutions or generalized trust. We also recognize, however, that reputations can be undeserved or out of date. Our preferences typically form a hierarchy: we prefer personal experience to a personal recommendation, and we prefer a personal recommendation to general reputation. One element in this is obvious: we trust our own judgement more than that of our friends or the general public. There is, however, more to it. There are two key advantages to dealing with someone we know. First, that person has an economic incentive to give us a good service in the hope of repeat business; and, if the service was good, we have an interest in paying promptly in order that he or she will want to deal with us again. It is a straightforward example of the market working to our mutual advantage. Second, in addition to the economic calculation there is also the question of social and personal ties, which create expectations of trust and make opportunistic exploitation immoral. This is the key point: we want to know not simply whether a trader is generally honest, but whether he or she will deal honestly *with us*.

Granovetter is not naïvely optimistic about the effectiveness of social networks in combating deceit and fraud. Social networks are often necessary to guarantee trustworthy behaviour, but they are not sufficient. Confidence tricksters can and do exploit them. Trust inevitably opens up the possibility of exploitation. Some crimes, typically financial fraud, can be committed only by people who have carefully built up networks of trust; Granovetter cites embezzlement as a prime example. Here the criminal may have spent years deliberately cultivating social networks, simulating trustworthiness in preparation for the sting.

Pyramid selling schemes provide another example of the manipulation of trust. Pyramid schemes imitate legitimate multi-level marketing operations, the key difference being that the latter have real products for sale to people who want to use them. Pyramid schemes either have no product at all, or, to give a semblance of legality and lend plausibility to the scam, they have a product of little value that is sold to people who buy it merely in order to sell it on down the line. The profit in pyramid schemes is made not by selling products but by recruiting new members who pay a fee to join.

It is easy to demonstrate that only a few people will make money, and that all such schemes are doomed to collapse. A simple illustration on the US Securities and Exchange Commission website shows why this is so (http://www.sec.gov/answers/pyramid.htm; accessed 05.03.2004). Imagine a pyramid scheme set up by six people, each of whom has to recruit six more people. At stage two in the scheme, therefore, thirty-six new members are brought in. By stage nine, the number of new people required has grown to over ten million, which is higher than the population of Chicago. By stage eleven, the figure required rises to over 360 million, which is more than the population of the United States. By stage thirteen, the number of new recruits needed is thirteen billion – twice the world's population. The arithmetic is simple, though the result is more extreme than most people would expect intuitively.

The appeal of such schemes includes, evidently, a desire to get rich quick. They often use crude high-pressure sales tactics, including the false claim that it is smart to jump on the bandwagon. Bogus testimonials from shills (allegedly satisfied participants) are a common tactic. These schemes feed on greed as well as ignorance; the market invariably punishes the latter but not necessarily the former.

Crucially, though, pyramid schemes often use social networks to exert moral pressure on potential recruits. A telling example is a pyramid selling scheme that flourished in the United Kingdom in the 1990s, initially under the name 'Women Empowering Women', and then later 'The Hearts' and 'The Circles'. This scam cleverly made a virtue of the fact that there was no product. Instead, women were asked to contribute a 'gift' of £3,000; when (if) they recruited eight people, they would themselves receive a 'gift' of £24,000. The scheme clothed itself in a rhetoric of feminism and sisterly comradeship; supporting literature spoke of 'the sacred female bond of trust and friendship'. Men were excluded from the scheme because they would crudely dismiss it as a device for making money, ignoring its caring aims. Recruiting friends and family was a loving thing to do. Critics who pointed out the fallacy of all pyramid schemes were righteously condemned as male cynics whose ingrained selfishness prevented them from recognizing the power of the women's movement. The heart would triumph over mathematics. Many of the people who took part undoubtedly believed this, to their cost.

Abandoned Markets, Abandoned Consumers

Financial services are intangible. They are not material goods that can be viewed, handled or given a test drive by potential purchasers. Savings, investments, loans and insurance are all about promises, many of which fall due only in the distant future, when consumers will find out whether their hopes have been fulfilled, disappointed or betrayed. Most consumers lack the cultural capital needed to evaluate financial products. Education in consumer finance has been low on the agenda of the state; ignorance is transmitted from generation to generation. Even for connoisseurs, evaluating financial services requires complex assessments of probabilities and risks. Many of the products are, and have been designed to be, opaque, so that they baffle even the experts. The culture of financial services is unashamedly promotional, blending information and hype into a seamless web. (As an illustration, I have found that financial service providers always claim that now is an ideal time to invest. When the stock market is rising, investors must not lose out on the gains to be made; when it is falling, there are bargains to be picked up cheaply; and when it is stagnant, careful stock-picking by their talented fund managers can secure profits for the wise. I have yet to discover when, according to these advisers, it would be a good time to sell.) Information asymmetries are rife: occasionally they benefit the consumer, who may, for example, have relevant knowledge about his or her health, lifestyle and life expectancy that can be concealed from insurance companies – though failure to disclose such information invalidates the policy, so insurers often have the last laugh. More commonly, it is the consumer who struggles to penetrate the smog of financial and legal jargon in the small print of the insurance contract. In most First World countries, responsibility for pensions is being transferred from the state and employers to individual citizens, whose need for accurate information and judicious advice is more pressing than ever. Poor people are financially excluded: the major financial institutions do not want them as clients, because they are seen as unreliable and anyway they do not generate enough profit, so they find themselves prey to the services of rapacious loan sharks and insurance scamsters. Even at the supposedly respectable end of the market, where affluent citizens are ripe to be 'cherry-picked', there is no shortage of financial advisers whose claims to professional competence, impartiality and integrity are questionable. Very often their income comes not from fees paid by the client but commission paid by the financial service provider. They are, in short, not advisers but salespeople.

Financial services have been prone to create markets that are *criminogenic*; they generate fraud as part of their normal functioning. The characteristics outlined in the previous paragraph are an invitation for fraud to flourish. It would appear to be a situation that demands tight regulation. Deregulation, however, is what the neoliberal agenda prescribes.

The offshore insurance industry (Tillman 2002, 2003) provides graphic examples of the impact of deregulation. In the late 1980s and early 1990s, many Californians found themselves in possession of worthless automobile insurance policies purchased from apparently sound companies with impressive titles, such as Union Pacific Fire and Marine. Unknown to most policy-holders, this company was based not in the United States but in the British Virgin Islands, a British Crown Dependency whose economy is totally dependent on its status as an offshore financial centre, more commonly known as a tax haven.

The crisis in California, Tillman explains, was brought about by two factors. First, legitimate insurance companies were driven from the market by a piece of legislation, initiated by voters and known as Proposition 103, which required insurance companies drastically to cut the premiums they were charging to customers in California. Voters believed that companies were making excess profits. The companies themselves decided, however, that Proposition 103 meant that they could no longer make sufficient profit from auto insurance in California, so they simply ceased to issue policies in the state.

At the same time, the second factor came into play: deregulation. In the United States, regulation of the insurance industry is not handled by the federal government but is largely left to each individual state. California's regulatory regime was already light; in the mid-1980s it was relaxed still further, on the neoliberal argument that government should not interfere in the operations of the free market. It was a fatal combination, a double abandonment of the market: flight of legitimate companies, and deregulation. Within the space of just three years, the sales of policies issued by unlicensed off-shore insurers rose fivefold. Only when policy-holders started to file claims did they discover that they had no cover and no redress. The market had been, in Tillman's words, 'abandoned', and consumers had been abandoned with it.

There is a third factor, which we shall examine in the final chapter of this book: globalization. In the globalized condition of high modernity, Giddens (1991) tells us, place has become 'phantasmagoric' – quite literally so, one might add, in the case of fictitious territories invented by fraudsters, such as the Principality of Sealand, the Principality of New Utopia and the Dominion of Melchizedek. From the standpoint of a defrauded investor holding a worthless insurance policy, there is no substantive difference between these fantasy countries and real ones such as the British Virgin Islands, where bogus international business corporations find a sanctuary from which to market their non-existent services. Offshore financial centres can offer a respectable front to dubious as well as legitimate financial services providers. To satisfy their financial clients, they should ideally be politically stable, economically sound, ostensibly democratic, and with loose links to a respectable First World country, typically the UK (Sikka 2003). Other British Crown Dependencies are Anguilla, Bermuda, the Cayman Islands, Gibraltar, Guernsey, the Isle of Man and Jersey. They offer the lightest of regulatory touches; the main condition in granting a licence usually is that the company does not sell its products in *their* territory.

Globalization has transformed financial markets across the world, unleashing a struggle between countries to gain an advantage in the global marketplace – a process aptly called 'competitive deregulation'. Justified in the name of consumer sovereignty, it can mean abandoning consumers to their fate.

Human Beings as Rational Actors

The prevalence of fraud invites questions about rationality. How can neoclassical economists cling to their strong claims about rationality in the face of the evidence?

Their response, as Pressberg (1998) argues, is to lay the blame on information asymmetry. Investors typically know less about goods and services than the people offering them, and even less about the motivations of the providers. Fraudsters know that they are fraudsters, but how can a potential investor distinguish them from honest traders? The problem, as we have seen, is particularly acute in the case of financial services, not least because promised returns usually lie some distance in the future, while payment is made now.

Rational choice theory implies that in this situation investors would be ultra-cautious. With their finances at stake, and knowing that information is highly asymmetric, rational investors would seek to obtain as much hard data as possible before deciding to invest. The more they stood to lose, and the more asymmetric the relationship, the more information they would seek. The remedy for potential market failure envisaged by neoclassical theory is that intermediary bodies such as consumer organizations will set up in the business of supplying objective information to investors. In addition, a legitimate role for the government is to support the market system by enacting legislation making it easier to detect fraud and punish it.

Unhappily for economic theory, this is not what usually happens. Far from engaging in a determined search for information, investors typically place their trust surprisingly easily in inflated prospectuses, bogus testimonials and worthless guarantees. They fail to ask elementary questions, and accept implausible and irrelevant assurances. They typically act not on a rational assessment of probabilities, but on faith.

A wealth of social-psychological literature, unjustifiably ignored by sociologists, has documented the ways in which decision-making departs from the canons of rationality. A lively overview of this complex material is provided by Sutherland (1992). Among the factors at work are the following:

Availability Error   We tend to base our judgements on what is 'available' to us, that is on what comes readily to mind. We are biased, for example, in favour of material that is dramatic, highly emotional, and concrete rather than abstract.

Primacy Error   It is widely recognized that first impressions count for a good deal; we interpret subsequent information in the light of our initial judgements, which we are reluctant to revise.

Recency Effect   Conversely, we tend to give more weight to new information than to old. When new material is closely connected with our initial impressions, the primacy effect operates; when it is disconnected, the recency effect applies.

Halo Effect   Our overall impression of a person is unduly influenced by one 'available' good trait; we generalize from this to the person's other characteristics, judging them to be better than they really are. (There is a converse 'devil' effect.)

Salience (Anchoring) Effect   We tend to give more weight to information that fits with our existing ideas than to information that fails to do so. This also means that we tend to seek information that confirms our beliefs in preference to information that might challenge them.

Sunk Cost Error   We have a tendency to throw good money after bad, refusing to cut our losses. It is a case of misplaced consistency; from a rational point of view, we should let go of our past errors and base our decisions on probable outcomes. Our attitudes to risk are inconsistent; it has been shown repeatedly that we are more inclined to take risks to save losses than to make gains.

Overconfidence   We routinely display misplaced confidence in our powers of judgement, in respect both of future events and of people's character. Since we rarely seek or recognize evidence that proves us wrong, our confidence is seldom shaken until disaster strikes.

Illusion of Control   This is a form of overconfidence; we believe we have control over events that are beyond it, including events due to pure chance. Gamblers are prone to this illusion. Many gamblers and a few croupiers believe that the croupier can determine where the roulette ball will fall; similarly, most dice players throw the dice softly if they want a low number and hard if they want a high one.

Social Conformity   Although we tend to value our independence of mind, we are greatly influenced by social pressures to conform with peer judgements and values and to obey authority, even in situations where to do so is manifestly irrational.

Poor Judgement of Probabilities   Our intuition is extremely unreliable in many situations that demand accurate estimates of probability. We are particularly poor at judging conditional probabilities, that is to say the probability that one thing is true, given that some other thing is true. A notorious illustration of this is a statistical phenomenon that was familiar to mathematicians in the nineteenth century, and has come to be known as the Monty Hall problem, after the host of an American television quiz show. In this quiz there were three doors on stage, labelled A, B and C. Behind one of these doors was a valuable prize, an automobile; behind each of the other two doors was a booby prize, a goat. Monty Hall knew in advance which door concealed the car and which other two hid a goat; the contestant, of course, did not know this. The contestant was asked to choose a door; say they chose door A. At this stage, we can all agree that the contestant has a one in three chance of winning the car. Monty would then open one of the other doors, say in this case door B, to show a goat. The contestant was then offered a choice: to stick with door A or switch to door C. What should they do?

A wealth of evidence, including my own experience of posing the problem to students and colleagues, shows that almost everyone agrees that it makes no difference whether the contestant sticks with their original choice of door A or switches to door C. We know that the car must be – and indeed is – behind one of these doors, so statistically the contestant has a one in two chance of winning it.

But we are all wrong. If the contestant switches, they double their chance of winning. The probability that the car is behind door A is one in three, but the probability that it is behind door C is two in three. There are various ways to show this; see, for example, the discussion in Stewart (1997: 69–98). Yet even after a proof has been demonstrated, many people refuse to accept it. My own experience indicates that the more senior the colleague, the less willing they are to accept any proof – which shows, among other things, that overconfidence is the fraudster's friend. Poor judgements of probabilities leave us wide open to being fleeced. And since markets depend on information, it is worth asking oneself: what new information has Monty Hall given us by showing the goat behind door B? What has he told us about door A? The answer is, nothing, which is why contestants who stick with door A still only have a one in three chance of winning the car. He has, however, given us information about door C: namely, that if there is a goat behind door A (which there will be on average two times out of three), then the second goat is behind door B *and the car is behind door C*. This is the valuable information he has given us, yet it is very hard to see it.

Perhaps the fate of a quiz show contestant does not matter unduly, but in other contexts faulty judgements of probability can be a matter of life or death. A particular difficulty surrounds inverse probability. If, say, a man has a test for prostate cancer, it is vital to distinguish two probabilities, each the inverse of the other: the probability, if you have prostate cancer, that you will test positive; and the probability, if you test positive, that you have prostate cancer. Our intuition may tell us that these two must be the same thing, but they are not. Unfortunately, tests for prostate cancer are currently unreliable. They give too many false negatives (false reassurance) and an even higher proportion of false positives (false alarms). It can be literally a matter of life and death, yet even doctors and researchers make serious mistakes in assessing conditional probabilities of this kind.

Finding Patterns in Chance Occurrences   We have a remarkable facility to find patterns in occurrences that are in fact due to random variations. An obvious case is the gambler's fallacy, also misleadingly known as the law of averages. A fair coin is tossed, and comes down 'heads' ten times in a row. Our intuition tells us that 'tails' is now far more likely; our reason will hopefully tell us that the coin has no memory, so that each toss carries an equal chance of heads or tails.

A less obvious case is the successful 'track record' of some managers of investment funds. Every year, as one would expect, some funds outperform the market while others underperform. As the years go by, some funds consistently outperform the market (these are the stars) while others consistently underperform (the dogs). In the former case, the company claims that its fund manager is a highly skilled investor; in the latter case, he or she gets the sack. Should we, then, invest in the successful funds and avoid the proven failures? Not if we accept the efficient market hypothesis, as discussed in chapter 2. According to the hypothesis, there is no rational way to beat the market. Outperformance, like underperformance, is simply a matter of chance. If so, the fact that some fund managers consistently perform well while others consistently perform badly does not prove the flair of the one and the incompetence of the other. If chance rules, we should expect some funds to do well or badly from year to year; this is not 'consistency', but the equivalent of heads coming up ten times in a row. It happens, but only by chance. We have discerned a pattern in sheer randomness, and concocted a spurious explanation of it.

Garfinkel provided a classic illustration of these processes (1967: 76–103). Student volunteers were told that they were taking part in a study to test new techniques of psychotherapy that might offer a constructive way of advising people about personal problems. Students were told to ask questions of the counsellor, who was located in another room and who would try to answer to the best of his ability, but, following the new techniques, would simply answer 'yes' or 'no' over an intercom. The reality was that the 'counsellor' was in fact an experimenter, whose answers were given entirely at random using a table of random numbers. This meant that there was no meaning intended in the answers, and no consistency; even so, the student volunteers typically constructed a meaning out of pure chance, and viewed the counselling as helpful.

The social-psychological evidence is devastating. Experiment after experiment has confirmed the effects cited above. Departures from rationality are significant, widespread and systematic. These were, admittedly, 'artificial' experiments; but they are confirmed by studying people's behaviour in social situations outside the laboratory. Personal finance provides a leading example. Stock markets are given to periodic fads, foibles and bubbles; investors buy when the market is booming, thereby purchasing shares when they are expensive, and sell in desperation when the market falls, thereby selling their shares cheaply; optimistic theories are flung together to explain why the world has changed so that everyone can be a winner; good money is regularly thrown after bad; people invest in schemes they do not understand; trust is readily placed in confidence tricksters; pyramid selling flourishes; people are confident that they can get rich quick, securing high rewards at no risk.

Nor is it simply a case of outrageous fraudsters duping a few fools. On the demand side, irrational financial decisions are widespread; on the supply side, dubious financial products are on offer from the major banks, insurance companies and investment houses. Many government-sponsored schemes have been no better.

The field of personal finance is what Wernick calls a promotional culture, by which he means 'a functionally interdependent complex within which the line between what is incidental as advertising and what is ostensibly its primary content, as information and entertainment, is reduced at most to a matter of level and degree' (Wernick 1991: 100). The financial services industry knows all about the availability error, the halo effect, overconfidence and the rest. Financial services are marketed so as to derive maximum benefit from these irrationalities. Regulatory agencies exist as much to bolster confidence in the market as to discipline service providers. Considered rationally, investors place too much trust in regulators. It is therefore naïve to think, as neoclassical economists do, that the problem is information asymmetry and that pumping as much information as possible into the system will solve it. In a fully-fledged promotional culture there is no such thing as information.

How are we to explain the pervasive failure of rationality? Fashionable if dubious answers to questions such as this are provided by evolutionary psychology. Compared to many predators, human beings are physically weak. Our survival as a species depended on joining with other humans; group conformity was therefore beneficial. In unexpected encounters with predators, our ancestors had to make an immediate decision between fight and flight. They had no time for a calm rational appraisal of all the options and their various probabilities; whatever else, a decision was needed quickly. Humans who relied on rough and ready shortcuts to help them decide what to do – what social psychologists call decision heuristics – were more likely to survive than those who opted for deep deliberations using the tools of probability theory.

Even if we accept such an explanation of the origins of irrationality, what accounts for its persistence? Surely there is an evolutionary advantage in acting rationally in a modern complex society, where investment scams and prostate cancer pose more of a threat than the sabre-toothed tiger? Perhaps the point is that these are problems requiring specialist treatment; the answer to them may lie in improved training of professionals and tighter regulation by professional bodies. For most of the decisions we make, departures from rationality are not fateful. The market offers us abundant choice, but much of it is trivial. More information, as recommended by neoclassical economics, will do less to promote human rationality than to bolster the allure of the market.

The fact that irrationality is endemic is further proof that the apparatus of economic theory fails to explain, as Parsons saw, how social order is possible. The evidence of systematic irrationality uncovered by social psychologists would be devastating *only if the market were as free marketeers depict it.*

Freedom and Autonomy

If the market does not guarantee rationality, does it deliver freedom? Neoliberal accounts of the market present it as a realm of individual liberty, whose freedoms are threefold. First, the individual as sovereign consumer is free to choose. Second, the consumer who chooses is also at liberty to reject; what the market offers is the freedom to exit. Third, freedom is essential negative: individuals are free from unwarranted interference by the state or other authorities. This negative conception of liberty is at the heart of classic liberalism running from John Locke and Adam Smith down to its twentieth-century formulation by Isaiah Berlin (1969).

It is not just liberals who acknowledge the power of the market to set people free from the constraints arbitrarily placed upon them by traditional societies. One of the undoubted historic achievements of commercial society was the liberation of individuals from roles and social positions ascribed at birth. Marx acknowledged this, as O'Neill points out (1998: 77–8). The development of market exchange destroyed the immutable status of feudal lord and vassal, landlord and serf. Although the free market of capitalism is, for Marx, an arena of alienation and class polarization, it is nevertheless the precondition of the full liberation of humanity to be accomplished by communism.

Despite their espousal of the concept of negative liberty, most advocates of the market are not libertarians; they recognize significant restrictions to the proper exercise of liberty. This points us to a crucial tension in liberal and neoliberal thought on what it is to be virtuous. Heelas (1991) expressed this tension succinctly in his analysis of Thatcherism. He distinguished a cast of four characters that were held up by Thatcherites as the key to virtue: *the enterprising self*, hardworking, self-reliant, willing to take calculated risks in pursuit of wealth-creation; *the sovereign consumer*, who actively seeks and rationally chooses goods and services offered through the market; *the active citizen*, who accepts personal responsibility for his or her life, and behaves responsibly towards other people; and *the conservative self*, law-abiding, self-disciplined, respectful of tradition and patriotic.

The divergent demands of these characters cannot easily be reconciled. The most blatant conflict is between the sovereign consumer, who is free to pursue her own wants through the market, and the conservative self, who is obliged to conform to the dictates of conventional morality (Thatcher's fictionally 'Victorian' values). For Giddens (1998: 15), the contradiction between dogmatic faith in the market and unbending commitment to traditional values and social institutions, supremely the family, is *the* fundamental fault line in neoliberal thought. The unfettered play of market forces tends to corrode traditional structures, not support them. Conservative values are not derived from market principles, but arbitrarily superimposed upon them. The specific case of Thatcherism illustrates a general principle: that neoliberal accounts of the market incorporate assumptions and prescriptions concerning the character of people who participate in the market. In all its variants, advocacy of the market claims that exposure to market forces is character-building.

There is a good case for arguing the exact opposite. The market system, and the consumer culture that accompanies it, destabilizes when it does not destroy the very institutions – family, community, occupation – in which character is formed and cherished. This is the dark side of the market's dynamism. Thus Richard Sennett's *The Corrosion of Character* (1998) argues that the world of work in the age of flexible specialization and incessant corporate re-engineering has brought a collapse of genuine commitment and loyalty, and their replacement by banal prattle about 'teams', vilification of experience, and the brute fact of constant surveillance and monitoring of performance. The decline of traditional occupational communities, and the rupture of cultural transmission from generation to generation, completes Sennett's portrait of the corrosive effect of the market on the virtues of character.

One might argue, as we saw in chapter 1 above, that postmodernist relativism is the ideal complement to the free market – a view taken by O'Neill. He writes scathingly of 'the unlovely figure loved by the postmodernist' (O'Neill 1998: 82), the idle *flâneur*, the conceited, self-indulgent loafer who plays narcissistically with his own identity and delights in connoisseurship of the fleeting pleasures on offer in the capital cities of Europe's old empires. This figure is a recent, and degenerate, incarnation of the Romantic hero. In glorifying his values, postmodernism wilfully dissolves the distinction between reality and appearance, a distinction without which the concept of character loses all meaning.

Rejecting the neoliberal analysis of liberty as inadequate and muddled, many writers, including those sympathetic to liberalism, have turned to a related concept: autonomy. The autonomous person is in control of her life; she has critically appraised her own cultural inheritance and her own endowments and dispositions. She steers a middle way between the two extremes of heteronomy and individualism. She is neither the slave of her culture and her inner drives, nor is she a narcissist who foolishly believes she is self-made.

According to Giddens the principle of autonomy informs most versions of emancipatory politics. In keeping with his philosophical position as a Third Way theorist (to be discussed below in chapter 4), Giddens thereby emphasizes the progressive nature of the theory. Equally notable is the fact that he links rights to responsibilities: 'Freedom and responsibility here stand in some kind of balance. The individual is liberated from constraints placed on her behaviour as a result of exploitative, unequal or oppressive conditions; but she is not thereby rendered free in any absolute sense. Freedom presumes acting responsibly in relation to others and recognising that collective obligations are involved' (Giddens 1991: 213).

Riesman argued the case for autonomy in his classic study, *The Lonely Crowd*. He distinguishes three character-types, each the product of particular types of society. Tradition-directed characters conform to social norms prescribed for people of their status group, whether class, caste, estate, gender or age; if they deviate, they are publicly shamed. Inner-directed characters are driven by norms and values implanted in them through socialization; if they deviate, they feel and are made to feel guilty. Other-directed characters strive to comply with the wishes of their peers; if they deviate, they feel anxiety.

A key point in Riesman's analysis is that each of these character-types is a victim of a type of conformity. Fortunately, the modern world offers autonomy as a fourth possibility, albeit one that can be achieved only through determined struggle. The autonomous person has the strength of character to resist demands to which the other character-types succumb: the freight of tradition, the hegemony of the superego and the burden of ontological insecurity.

The neoliberal analysis of freedom is deeply contradictory. Negative liberty, as in classical liberalism, appears to be its bedrock; yet this is typically coupled with an endorsement of character virtues whose nurturing depends upon non-market and even anti-market institutions, notably kinship, community, ethnicity, religion and education.

Money and Monies

To economists, money is a homogeneous, featureless, infinitely divisible medium of exchange and store of value. These qualities are its virtues; they make the market possible. To sociologists, from the classical foundations laid by Marx, Weber and Simmel to contemporary contributions by Giddens and Habermas, money has precisely the same characteristics – except that they are not seen as virtues.

Following Zelizer (1997: 1–12) we can identify a number of interrelated themes in the sociological critique of money.

Instrumentality

Money is a means to an end, acting as a store of value but having little or no value in its own right. It is, as Simmel said (1990/1907), the purest reification of means. Money's unconditional interchangeability makes it the ideal medium of exchange in a market society. It represents the triumph of a calculative, instrumentally rational approach to life, the victory of *Gesellschaft* over *Gemeinschaft*. Simmel pointed out that money is the appropriate medium of exchange between prostitutes and their clients, since their relationship involves a shared indifference to each other as human beings, a 'mutual degradation to a mere means'. Generalizing from this, he claimed that there is in the nature of money itself something of the essence of prostitution.

Quantification

Since it is featureless, money is essentially quantitative rather than qualitative. All money is fundamentally the same; only the amount varies. Money's infinite divisibility makes it a perfect medium for arithmetic calculation. To Simmel, money symbolizes the reduction of quality to quantity, a defining feature of the modern world.

The Profane

According to Durkheim, the social world is sharply divided between two spheres: the sacred, which contains things that are set apart and forbidden to ordinary mortals, and the profane, the world in which we carry out our everyday business. Featureless, quantified, utilitarian: money clearly belongs to the profane world.

Commodification

Through the power of money, all manner of social transactions are inexorably drawn into the web of the market. The effect is to corrupt and dehumanize social relationships; personal ties are replaced by calculative contracts, and spiritual values are extinguished by materialistic urges. Expressed most powerfully by Marx – for whom money was 'a god among commodities' – the commercialization of society and commodification of social relationships has been a recurrent theme in critiques of modernity. Lacking any meaning of its own, money degrades everything by putting a price on it.

Rationalization

Max Weber and the other classical sociologists saw the expansion of money as a key agent of the process of rationalization. Money is colourless, heartless, quantity without quality. In economists' terms it is fungible, that is to say, it is replaceable by itself. One dollar bill is no different from any other: irrespective of where the individual note came from or where it is bound for, what matters is that it represents the power to purchase, at current prices, one dollar's worth of goods and services – nothing more, nothing less. Zelizer (1997: 7) points out that for Simmel, as for other classical sociologists, the view that money might be 'cursed' or 'stained with blood' was a dying superstition of no consequence in the modern world. (They clearly had not anticipated the convoluted transactions implicated in money laundering, through which criminals seek to erase all trace of the source of their illegal wealth.) On a Simmelian view, market money is the only form of money there is.

Zelizer's aim is to challenge this orthodoxy, using case studies of the uses of money in the United States between 1870 and 1930. She demonstrates that the federal authorities had great difficulty creating a centralized uniform legal tender based on the greenback dollar (Zelizer 1997: 13–18). Rival currencies, such as those issues by individual states, as well as silver and gold certificates (yellowbacks) were gradually suppressed in the wake of the 1862 National Banking Act. Even when, in the twentieth century, standardization of the currency was officially accomplished (it was formally ratified by Congress as late as 1933), this aspect of nation building did not amount to cultural homogenization.

In everyday social life, people continue to draw distinctions between different monies depending on their provenance and their purposes. Money is socially shaped and earmarked in a variety of ways. Its uses may be restricted: gifts of money may be expected to be used for specific purposes, such as purchasing clothes for special occasions rather than paying the grocery bill (a birthday present meant to finance a treat, not a necessity) or clearing gambling debts rather than going out for a meal (a loan not intended to support further extravagance). Monies may be physically separated for designated purposes in envelopes, jars and piggy banks. Money can be paid as a gratuity to a waiter or cab driver, but not to a professional. The transfer of money is often ritualized; for example, in traditional working-class families in the UK, men would often leave their wife's housekeeping allowance under an ornament on the mantelpiece, instead of handing it over directly as an unadorned payment for services rendered. Responsibilities for particular expenditures are often allocated in conventional ways: a woman buys the children's clothes, while her husband pays for family holidays.

If money were featureless, a household's monetary assets could be deployed flexibly as convenience dictated. For example, the coins painstakingly amassed in a child's piggy bank to pay for a pet rabbit could be used by her father to purchase, say, his weekly supply of cigarettes. Where would the harm be if repayment were made, especially with interest? Yet in nearly all families such behaviour would be regarded as a sign of weakness of character, even depravity. Ironically, as Zelizer comments, academic sociology has been blind to the richness of popular conceptions and uses of money. If we ask why sociologists, like economists, have clung to their misguided (and impoverished) interpretations of money, a large part of the explanation must be the powerful myth of the market.

In the nineteenth century, cash donations to the poor were seen as dangerous. Poor people were morally deficient, and so would waste the cash on frivolous self-indulgence. Gifts in kind, such as food, fuel and clothing, enabled donor agencies to exert some control over the lives of the poor, and so were the preferred way of transferring resources to alleviate poverty. Towards the beginning of the twentieth century, a significant change took place in the way poor people were viewed by the authorities. Transferring cash to the poor gradually came to be seen as progressive and liberating, unlike demeaning charitable gifts, which robbed them of the capacity to choose. The problem with poor people was not moral but technical; the poor were thought to be incompetent spenders. Concern focused on poor women, above all recent immigrants to the United States. Armed with the science of home economics, the role of social workers was redefined as educating the poor in the principles of rational consumption. Social workers fulfilled their new professional project by emphasizing the impersonality of money; cash relief was to be treated as simply a wage paid by the state. Poor people were expected to fill out official forms accounting for their expenditure, so that they could be instructed how to spend their money wisely. Progressive in intent, this insistence on market money legitimated professional intrusion into the domestic sphere. It met with determined resistance, not least because it violated the norms and values that govern the definition, distribution and allocation of domestic monies.

Although it is clear that Zelizer's work represents a celebration of the diversity of social life and the inventiveness of the human spirit, she is aware of the need to address uncomfortable questions. Perhaps the creative cultural and social diversity she has uncovered is no more than a desperate attempt to humanize money, putting a sentimental gloss on a harsh reality. Part of that reality must be the exercise of power. As she recognizes (1997: 210), 'the accounts of domestic, gift, and charitable monies leave no doubt that separate currencies have repeatedly served to enforce the dependency of women, children, and the poor'. It is not just intimacy and commitment but inequality that is signalled in these transactions; men do not have pin money, the middle classes would be affronted by food stamps, and academics do not receive gratuities (though their universities solicit donations).

Zelizer's work encourages us to abandon the assumption that money is a uniquely neutral medium. Instead, it should be analysed as carrying symbolic messages, just as other commodities do. Money is, admittedly, more resistant to personalization than material objects; it is more fungible, mobile and transferable. Her conclusion is telling. If rationalization were rampant, market money would be universal. Yet this is not so; 'instead, the constant, vigorous, and pervasive differentiation of modern monies provides the most powerful evidence *against* a homogenized, instrumental model of social life' (Zelizer 1997: 214).

In *Spheres of Justice*, Michael Walzer uses the term 'blocked exchanges' to refer to types of monetary transaction that are banned from the market. He provides a list, which he claims is exhaustive, of fourteen categories of blocked exchange in the contemporary United States (Walzer 1983: 100–03):

1 Slavery is illegal: human beings cannot be bought and sold, only their labour power can be.
2 Political power and influence cannot be bought and sold; bribery is illegal. Nor can citizens sell their votes.
3 Criminal justice is not for sale; judges and juries cannot be bribed.
4 The freedoms of speech, of the press, of religion, and of assembly are guaranteed to every citizen and do not have to be paid for.
5 Marriage and procreation rights are not for sale; polygamy is illegal.
6 The right to emigrate from the political community is not for sale.
7 Exemptions from military service, jury service and other citizen duties cannot be purchased.
8 Political offices cannot be bought; were it so, it would be a secular form of simony – the purchase of an office in the Church.
9 Basic welfare services such as police protection and education up to school-leaving age are provided free at the point of consumption.

10   Desperate exchanges or 'trades of last resort' are prohibited; people are protected by legislation laying down minimum wages, maximum hours, and health and safety requirements.
11   Various prizes and honours cannot be bought and sold, but are awarded on merit.
12   Divine grace cannot be bought or sold. (As Walzer wryly remarks, this is not just because God does not need the money, since his ministers may feel that *they* do.)
13   Love and friendship cannot be bought and sold.
14   Criminal transactions cannot by definition be conducted legally.

The list obviously encompasses a wealth of detailed case law. It is the product of the history of a civilization; formulating, enacting and policing the rights and duties enshrined in these fourteen principles is a massive cultural undertaking, and subject to continual contestation – as witnessed by contemporary controversies over the purchase of human organs, children for adoption and surrogate mothers. If the list of proscriptions is testimony to the power of money, it also bears witness to the massive cultural investment in creating a boundary around the market, to prevent it from colonizing the whole of society.

Sociological critiques of money, supremely those mounted by Marx and Engels and by Simmel, tend to treat money as possessing an intrinsic, magical power to revolutionize social relationships. Ironically, as Parry and Bloch comment (1989: 3), money is in danger of being fetishized as much by critical scholars as by stockbrokers.

Primitive and Modern Economies

A theme of this chapter, and indeed of the whole book, is that 'the market' is a myth that feeds the Western imagination. One aspect of the myth has already been touched on several times: the contrast between the dynamic free-market economies of the liberal-democratic capitalist West and the stagnant command economies of state socialism.

Another and more ambivalent contrast has been no less compelling; here, the Other is represented by 'primitive' economies.

A series of dichotomies is presented (Parry and Bloch 1989: 7): we are modern, they are traditional; we produce for exchange, they produce for use; we have commodities, they have gifts; we are calculative, they are innocent of calculation; we have market money, they do not.

For many years, economic anthropology was dominated by a debate between formalism and substantivism. The formal approach to the economy treats the analytic concepts developed by Western economics as universal in application. Primitive economies are no less governed than their industrial counterparts by instrumental rationality, the calculation of efficient means to achieve one's ends, involving a cost–benefit analysis in the context of resources which are by definition scarce. The substantive approach rejects the universal application of Western economic analysis, and treats 'primitive' economies as having their own distinctive character which will be discovered by empirical enquiry, not defined by a priori theories. This controversy within economic anthropology is an instance of a more general problem about Western categories and their application. Are they context- and culture-free? And could any concept be so?

A classic, polemical source in the debate is Karl Polanyi's *The Great Transformation*, which propounded the substantivist position. Polanyi distinguished three principles that govern exchange. Although he recognized that these could co-exist in a society, he nevertheless argued that societies will typically be dominated by one of them.

Reciprocity is characteristic of small-scale, decentralized, egalitarian societies, as in Melanesia. Gift-giving creates complex networks of interpersonal reciprocal obligations into which all members of the society are incorporated. Reciprocity, Polanyi argues, is supported by 'the institutional pattern of symmetry', a form of social organization appropriate to fostering egalitarian relations between partners.

Redistribution is not an egalitarian but a hierarchical principle, and as such was characteristic of feudal societies. Members of the society are obliged to transfer goods to a powerful central authority, whether a tribal chief or a state administration, which then redistributes them within the society. Such a system is supported by 'the institutional pattern of centrality', which confers legitimacy on the regime.

These two forms of distribution are radically different from the principle that governs industrial societies: the *market* principle. Because the market is based on formally 'free', abstract, impersonal, monetary contracts between the various parties to an exchange, it has the capacity to provide social integration for large-scale and widely dispersed societies. The market system differs from reciprocity and redistribution in one crucial respect: 'instead of economy being embedded in social relations, social relations are embedded in the economic system' (Polanyi 1957/1944: 57).

Adam Smith believed, as Polanyi reminds us, that humans have by nature an inborn propensity 'to truck, barter, and exchange one thing for another' (1976/1776: 25). Polanyi's judgement on this is decisive (1957/1944: 43): 'In retrospect it can be said that no misreading of the past ever proved more prophetic of the future.' What Smith saw as a natural trait of all human beings is a specific product of market society. This argument was taken up by Sahlins, as discussed in chapter 1 above. Western economics is a product of Western material prosperity; ironically, 'it was not until culture neared the height of its material achievements that it erected a shrine to the Unattainable: *Infinite Needs*' (Sahlins 1972: 39).

On Gudeman's interpretation, 'primitive' societies are based on the community economy (Gudeman 1986). In such an economy, production is geared not to market exchange but to consumption by the individual or group. The aim is not the accumulation of wealth but the reproduction of a way of life, one that is deeply rooted in a particular place, a landscape and climate cherished in collective memory. A community economy has a shared 'commons', a base that can include land, crops, tools, ancestors, spirits and ceremony. Ideally at least, the community economy is founded on trust, mutual dependence, and a fundamental equality.

Gifts play a crucial role in such economies, as shown in Marcel Mauss's classic study (1954/1925) of Melanesian societies. In a gift relationship, the parties have a threefold obligation: to make gifts, receive them, and repay them in a suitable way at the proper time. The objects exchanged do not have a price, as they necessarily do in a market economy; instead, they carry with them the identity of the giver, so that in accepting a gift the recipient also accepts or confirms a social relationship to the donor. The exchange of gifts is a discontinuous expression of generous acts that create a network of diffuse reciprocal obligations embracing the whole of a society. Mauss emphasizes the significance within gift economies of what he calls *prestations totales*, exchanges through which 'all kinds of institutions find simultaneous expression: religious, legal, moral, and economic' (Mauss 1954/1925: 1).

Commenting on Mauss's analysis, Bourdieu underlines the significance of the interval between gift and countergift. Returning a gift too quickly is a symbolic affront, because it implies a calculative approach in which the return gift becomes a mere payment, thus refusing to accept the gift by redefining it as a service within a market economy. The time interval is necessary in order that both donors and recipients can experience a gift as a gift. The longer and less determinate the socially sanctioned interval between receiving a gift and reciprocating, the more the interaction is constituted and experienced as disinterested.

On one interpretation, an immediate reciprocation would reveal the 'true' nature of the gift relationship. This supposed truth is that gift relationships are based on self-interest; they are simply a form of market exchange, subject like any other to calculations of personal advantage. As Bourdieu puts it (1998a: 121): 'The economistic logic of rational action suggests the following reality: "I know that you know that I know that you will reciprocate".' It is 'common knowledge' that there is no such thing as a pure gift freely given without expectation of a return; to believe otherwise is at best a sentimental delusion, and at worst rank hypocrisy.

Bourdieu argues that we should reject the 'official cynicism' displayed by such economistic analysis of the truth of gift relationships. Instead, he proposes that the logic of gift exchange is as follows (1998a: 121): ' "I am the way I am, disposed in such a way that I know and do not want to know that you know and do not want to know that I know and do not want to know that you will give me a countergift".' This 'not wanting to know' is an essential ingredient of the gift relationship. It is not a denial of the truth, nor an act of psychological repression, nor hypocrisy, but a social fact, a taboo on not revealing the *illusio*, the open secret that we co-operate to maintain. We have no wish to make everything explicit, as if that were necessary or desirable. The price system works to render value explicit; and for that very reason we cut the price tags off the gifts we give. In refusing the logic of price, we refuse the lived reality of calculation and calculability (Bourdieu 1998a: 96–7).

Just as self-interest is not the reality, nor is altruism. We are socialized to be generous, within a culture 'in which countergifts and other rewards are collectively expected to be forthcoming' (Bourdieu 2000: 192). Gift relationships are not necessarily benign; they can lock people into subordination and exploitation. In such cases, the introduction of market relationships, and specifically payment in cash, can be a liberation. Recognizing the ambivalence of gift exchange, Bourdieu's approach attempts to transcend the false choice between cynicism and sentimentality.

Davis argues that, at least when we theorize about it, we typically overstate the part played by commerce in contemporary society, thereby falling victim to a crude stereotype. The contrast with 'primitive' society fuels the stereotype; our portrait of them is prone to exaggeration and romanticism (Parry and Bloch 1989). We paint them as innocent of calculation in order to point up our own selfishness. We treat their gifts as 'pure', whereas ours are sullied by self-interest. We play down the significance of money in 'primitive' economies, so that money can be presented as the acid that has corroded community.

Economic analysis notwithstanding, it is questionable whether 'pure' market exchanges are dominant in modern societies. Davis draws attention to the rich repertoire of exchange; he lists forty-two types of exchange in operation in contemporary Britain (1992: 29): alms-giving, altruism, arbitrage, banking, barter, bribery, burglary, buying/selling, charity, commodity-dealing, corruption, donation, employment, exploitation, expropriation, extortion, futures trading, giving, huckstering, insider dealing, insurance, marketing, money-lending, mortgaging, mugging, pawning, profiteering, prostitution, reciprocity, renting, retailing, robbery, scrounging, shoplifting, shopping, simony, social wage, swapping, theft, tipping, trading and wholesaling.

This list not intended to be anything like complete; it is quite easy to think of omissions such as nepotism, patronage, pimping, procuring, sponsorship, subsidy and trafficking. It does not include a vast number of technical terms unique to particular domains and well known only to participants in that field. As a flavour of such terms it includes simony, the sinful purchase of a spiritual office in the Church; in the Church of England, all clergy are required to make a formal Declaration Against Simony before they take up a new office. Nor does the list, as Davis points out, contain qualified terms such as *child* prostitution or *armed* robbery, qualifications which draw vital distinctions signalling degrees of approval or condemnation.

A crucial point about this repertoire is that it involves not just the economic exchange of goods and services, but social relationships infused with legal, moral or religious meaning. At a conservative estimate, fifteen of the terms are obviously pejorative and four positive. They are also marked by considerable ambivalence, as shown the various connotations of 'charity'.

Boiling all these subtle differences down to a simple pair, buying and selling, would ignore the complexity of social life and the subtlety of people's interpretations of it. Davis rightly remarks (1992: 46) that our understanding of what it is to live a full life and be a rounded person 'leads us to attempt to play a number of different pieces from the repertoire available'. To achieve this ideal, we may strive to be 'market-wise in commerce, reciprocal with our friends, a little bit charitable, and altruistic up to a point'.

A tired joke among economists is to point out – quite correctly – that if a man marries his housekeeper, ceases to pay her a wage but instead gives her 'housekeeping money', the wealth of the nation decreases. Conversely, one might add, if wives divorced their husbands and demanded proper payment for domestic services, the nation would become far wealthier. The reason for these perverse effects is that only a limited number of transactions are entered into the national accounts. The exclusions and inclusions are revealing evidence of official discourses; it would be extremely naïve to mistake the accounts for objective reality. Most of the exchanges we make with friends and relatives escape the official accounting procedures; if we ignore them, we shall produce a lop-sided account of social life that inevitably emphasizes quantification of outputs rather than quality of relationships.

The 'Problem' of Culture

Zelizer (2002) distinguishes three broad approaches to culture in sociological analyses of the economy. What she calls *extension* is the application of mainstream economic analysis to 'cultural' areas of social life that economics has neglected. As noted in chapter 2, Becker's *The Economic Approach to Human Behaviour* (1976) is a paradigm case of this approach, in which rational choice theory is applied to the markets in crime, marriage and the family, and 'racial' discrimination. In this school of thought, culture is treated as the pattern of consumer preferences; these are taken as 'given' and no attempt is made to explain them.

The second approach is to treat culture as a *context* that facilitates or constrains economic action. Following Polanyi (1957/1944) and Granovetter (1985), this approach sees economic phenomena as *embedded* in social processes. In Granovetter's work the emphasis is placed on social networks in deliberate contrast to cultural values; the reason is that Granovetter was reacting against Parsonian sociology's high degree of abstraction and emphasis on an overarching societal value-system. It was no doubt salutary to reject those forms of degenerate Parsonianism in which values are free-floating and explain everything. Equally necessary was the critique of economists' treatment of culture as a God of the Gaps, invoked when rational explanations fail.

In retrospect, for all its fertility Granovetter's approach was, as he acknowledges, an over-reaction. Its legacy has been the treatment of culture as of secondary importance, and at times as little more than an afterthought. In so far as economic sociologists have tended to adopt this approach, they have made too many concessions to the agenda and paradigm of neoclassical economics.

Zelizer advocates a third *alternative* approach, in which the aim is neither to extend nor to contextualize economic analysis but to challenge it. As an illustration of what is involved in the alternative approach, consider the following:

> 'For my part I don't see why men who have got wives and don't want 'em, shouldn't get rid of 'em as these gipsy fellows do their old horses,' said the man in the tent. 'Why shouldn't they put 'em up and sell 'em by auction to men who are in need of such articles? Hey? Why, begad, I'd sell mine this minute if anybody would buy her!'

In this defining scene in Thomas Hardy's *The Mayor of Casterbridge* (1886), the novel's central character, Michael Henchard, under the influence of rum and his vindictive temper, sells his wife and daughter at a country fair for the sum of five guineas. It is a shocking event, with fateful repercussions. Sociologically, it raises three aspects of the cultural dimension of economic action: in Spillman's words (1999: 1), 'the cultural construction of objects of market exchange, the cultural construction of the parties to market exchange, and the cultural construction of norms of exchange'. What can legitimately be exchanged, by whom can it be bought and sold, and according to what social rules? In answering these questions, as shown by Thomas Hardy's example of a man selling his wife, we need to examine inequalities of power between the parties concerned (Davis 1992: 37–46).

The social construction of a market involves multiple interactions between a variety of actors pursuing their own interests and values. Creating a new market is a struggle, as Zelizer (2001) demonstrates in her work on the market for life insurance in the United States. From the beginning of the nineteenth century, there was a general trend towards rationalizing the management of death. It included investing in life insurance, making a will and organizing a funeral. Although these are widely regarded nowadays as not only prudent but also morally good things to provide for, they initially met fierce resistance. Commercializing death, turning it into a money-making business, was seen as dirty work; death should be an intimate family and neighbourhood affair. Putting death on the market offended the sanctity of human life, and inserted the market, an irredeemably profane set of activities, into the sacred realm. After the 1840s, resistance to rationalization collapsed. Zelizer offers four sets of cultural developments that account for this. Taken together they show just how much cultural work underpinned the success of rationalization.

First, religious opposition was gradually overcome. To traditionalists, life insurance was a sacrilegious interference with God's dispensation. The Lord giveth, and the Lord taketh away; widows and orphans lay in his divine care, as entrusted to his church(es). Modernizers argued in contrast that God looks favourably on those who make suitable provision for their heirs and dependants, and that their virtue would live on in the loving memory of their beneficiaries.

Second, risk and speculation were reconceptualized. Life insurance was not a form of gambling; a widow who benefited from her husband's prudent foresight was not the unworthy winner of a lottery, profiting from an unearned windfall. Life insurance was transformed from speculation to wise investment. As part of this rethinking, superstitious reasoning had to be surmounted, namely the fear that by making provision for one's death one might magically bring it about. Arguably, such fears have not been wholly defeated, which may be a reason why so many people fail to make a will and die intestate.

Third, the growing urbanization of America brought changes in the kinship system. As community and the extended family system declined, so the burden of care for widows and orphans fell on the nuclear family. Informal systems of support atrophied, so bureaucratic and professional systems stepped in to fill the breach. Life insurance was part of this wider trend.

Finally, changing attitudes towards life and death played a crucial part. Resistance to life assurance appealed to the principle that no monetary value can be placed on human life. As Zelizer argues (2001: 151) life insurance shattered this taboo, becoming 'the first largescale enterprise in America to base its entire organization on the accurate estimate of the price of death'.

The example of life insurance illustrates that commodification is contested, and depends upon complex processes of reframing. Another example is debt. Bell (1979) points out that banks successfully transformed socially stigmatized 'debt' into socially acceptable 'consumer credit'. Until the 1920s, people had to purchase goods out of income or savings. From that time on, banks began to lend money to private individuals as well as to businesses. The destigmatization of debt was a necessary precondition of the expansion of consumer credit – itself a necessary precondition of the rise of consumer society.

Marketing life insurance and consumer credit involved more than overcoming resistance; it was a creative process of framing the parties, objects and norms of exchange. Adam Smith believed that human beings have a natural propensity to engage in market exchanges – a position that overlooks the cultural work needed to fashion individuals as suitable participants in a given market.

If life insurance and consumer credit are examples of the successful legitimation of once-discreditable activities, prostitution provides a contemporary instance of the opposite, as campaigners seek to stigmatize the clients of workers in the sex trade. The complexities of campaigns to 'penalize the buyers' are vividly brought out by O'Connell Davidson (2003). A key factor that is obscured by such campaigns is the role of the state in creating and perpetuating the social conditions – poverty, subordination of women to men, toleration of violence against women, racism, and hostility to immigrants – that favour the growth of prostitution and the global sex trade. State agencies and their employees are all too often among the main violators of prostitutes' human rights and dignity. Given this, it is naïve to call upon the state as an innocent, neutral partner in the struggle against the commercial sexual exploitation of women. Penalizing the buyers can easily distract attention from the problems of the sex workers themselves, most of which stem from their callous treatment as mere commodities. Reinforcement of their rights as workers would often prove more effective than campaigns of stigmatization that run against the grain of cultures in which purchasing sex is taken for granted as normal market behaviour.

As a final example of the cultural work need to create markets and socialize actors for participation in them, I shall consider consumer organizations and the field of personal finance. I have argued elsewhere (Aldridge 1994) that consumer organizations do more than carry out their ostensible mission of supplying objective information to consumers – the role prescribed by neoclassical economics as a counter to market failure caused by information asymmetry. Consumer organizations help to create the rational consumer: a person who is goal-oriented, forward-looking, disciplined, time-consistent and ascetic. Far from being self-indulgence, as Daniel Bell (1979) would have it, this is the Protestant ethic revamped. Consumption is serious work, and people have to be prepared for it.

One arena in which this is apparent is the market for personal financial services (Aldridge 1997, 1998). There is a vast body of self-help literature whose superficial purpose, in line with the official goals of consumer organizations, is to arm potential investors with the objective information they need in order to make rational investment decisions. Strikingly, however, they do not do so. What they do instead is: encourage readers to take responsibility for their personal finances; stress the need for professional financial advice; direct readers to the sources through which reputable professional advice is available; provide reassurance that industry regulation is highly effective; and characterize the professional–client relationship as an unthreatening, non-deferential service encounter in which clients can participate with confidence. They are, in short, a vehicle of adult socialization. In a period during which the field of personal finance has been shaken by a series of scandals, the work they perform – and it is a struggle – is to create a clientele for the financial services industry.

The crucial role played by professional financial advisers may point to an unexpected conclusion. As we saw in the discussion of money, everything associated with the market is typically seen as belonging to the realm that Durkheim defined as profane in contrast to sacred. The category of the profane is not entirely clear in Durkheim's thought; the only agreed factor is that he saw it as one side of a dichotomy. Thus the profane may mean things that are mundane, lacking in symbolic meaning, materialistic, utilitarian and rational. On the other side of the dichotomy stands the sacred: a realm of things set apart and forbidden, things which are symbolically charged and approachable only through rituals. The sacred is not necessarily benign. Durkheim argues that it has a negative pole; Lucifer and his equivalents belong there. Good or evil, auspicious or inauspicious, the sacred is dangerous to mortals.

From this point of view, the market too can be a dangerous place; why else should the buyer beware? Hence, for example, the cultural effort that is needed to persuade people to invest in the stock market. Hence too the need for professional financial advisers; they are ritual specialists who put ordinary investors in touch with the sacred. Hence too the celebration of such charismatic figures as Peter Lynch, who for the thirteen years between 1977 and 1990 managed Fidelity's lucrative Magellan fund, which grew to have over a million shareholders and some $14 billion of assets; or Warren Buffett, the 'Oracle of Omaha', investment guru to the little guy.

According to Khurana (2002), a fundamental transition, which began in the 1980s, is taking place as managerial capitalism gives way to investor capitalism. The trend is most evident in the USA, but is spreading to other Western societies. Many more people than before hold stock market investments, which have become a crucial ingredient in planning for retirement. Partly for this reason, the press and television give unprecedented coverage to stock markets and the performance of companies quoted on them. The tendency of the mass media to 'personalize' events leads them to focus on the role of charismatic Chief Executive Officers, the corporate leaders who turn companies around (or bring them to their knees). The CEO is a contemporary celebrity, and as such has become the object of a quasi-religious cult. Their high 'fat cat' salaries and lucrative share options can be interpreted in this light, not as performance-related pay but as a tribute sacrificially offered to them by ordinary mortals.

When a corporation wants to hire a new CEO, the trend is to look to make an appointment from outside the firm. This, I would argue, is entirely in keeping with a Weberian perspective on charisma. The charismatic leader is socially constructed as not like common humanity; often his or her origins are shrouded in mystery (a miraculous birth, for example). Just as charismatic movements flourish in times of social upheaval, so it is corporations that are in crisis that look to appoint somebody from outside to reverse their fortunes. Their problems may be structural, but they are committed to the irrational belief that every problem has a hero who can solve it. As the title of Khurana's book signals, they are looking for *a corporate saviour*.

If this is so, then Weberian theory would suggest that the search cannot be conducted on rational lines. The quest for a charismatic leader is ritualized and symbolically charged; only through ritual and symbolism can charisma be transmitted from a leader to his or her successor. The mechanisms of the rational search – advertisements, short-listing committees, aptitude tests, a programme of interviews – are not appropriate means for discovering a charismatic leader; no religious movement uses such techniques to find its new spiritual head.

So it is with the search for a charismatic CEO. A company is likely to know far less about an outsider than about its own employees. Interviews are a notoriously poor method of selection, as countless psychological experiments have conclusively shown, yet companies rely on them. The interview is an exceedingly brief encounter; nevertheless, as Khurana found, most directors believe that they have the ability to discern a person's leadership qualities very quickly indeed. What they describe is not so much a rational search, based on full information, but a *coup de foudre*, or love at first sight. This is not a rational market but a hermetically closed culture, in which an elite of putatively charismatic saviours circulates among bands of disciples. 'Restricting the CEO labor market to a select set of candidates and then pretending that the outcomes can be justified as a consequence of the market process is', as Khurana comments (2002: 206), 'a self-serving conceit'.

Treating the market as 'profane' is an expression of the view that it is devoid of culture, and thus the sort of activity that is suitable for economic analysis. But all economic action and all markets are intrinsically cultural; there is no such thing as culture-free action. Slater (2002: 59) puts the point sharply: 'in practice, social actors cannot actually define a market or a competitor, let alone act in relation to them, except through extensive forms of cultural knowledge'. Without shared understandings, the market could not even be recognized, let alone function. To believe that markets are somehow free from culture is to fall victim to the pervasive ideology that the market is an elemental force of nature.

4
Colonization, Compromise and Resistance

> To the degree that the economic system subjects the life-forms of private households and the life conduct of consumers and employees to its imperatives, consumerism and possessive individualism, motives of performance, and competition gain the force to shape behaviour. The communicative practice of everyday life is one-sidedly rationalized into a utilitarian lifestyle; this media-induced shift to purposive-rational action orientations calls forth the reaction of a hedonism freed from the pressures of rationality. (Habermas 1987: 325)

In those two sentences from the second volume of his *Theory of Communicative Action*, Jürgen Habermas summons up the spectre of colonization that haunts so many of the market's critics. They are afraid that the market will break free of its proper boundaries and invade other territories to which it is anathema. Imperialism may be an inbuilt tendency of the market – a position adopted in some of the literature on globalization. This interpretation tends to fatalism, for if the market is an elemental force then perhaps it is irresistible. Other analysts treat marketization as a political project pursued by the market's advocates. This position invites the question, how can the project of marketization be opposed?

Beck's Critique of Globalism

In *What is Globalization?*, Ulrich Beck (2000) distinguishes three related terms: globalization, globality and globalism. *Globalization* refers to 'the processes through which sovereign national states are criss-crossed and undermined by transnational actors with varying prospects of power, orientations, identities and networks' (Beck 2000: 11). The trend cannot be reversed; there is no way back to the haven of the sovereign nation-state. The destination of this process is *globality*, a 'world society' that encompasses 'the totality of social relationships which are not integrated into or determined (or determinable) by national-state politics' (2000: 10). Globality means multiplicity without unity, and involves a transformation in social consciousness. So it is that for many sociologists the discipline needs a radically overhauled agenda, one which takes fully into account the fluidity of the new world order (Bauman 2000; Castells 2000; Urry 2000) and the decline of the traditional supports of personal identity and the social fabric.

While urging us to face up to the shock of the new, Beck rejects *globalism*, the ideology of neoliberalism which declares that the world market has eliminated the need for or possibility of political action. Globalism touts a crushingly simplistic explanation of globality, reducing the complex process of globalization to one dimension, the economic. All other domains – ecology, culture, politics, civil society – are represented as being determined by the logic of the market. Beck repeatedly characterizes globalism as a 'thought-virus' that has penetrated all the major social institutions, not least political parties and the media. Its thrust is anti-political; individual actors and social movements are simply the vehicles of the operation of the world market laws – thus conveniently ignoring the politics of the major global players, such as the World Bank, the World Trade Organization, the International Monetary Fund, the Organization for Economic Co-operation and Development, and the giant transnational corporations.

If no resistance is mounted to the ideology and practice of globalism, the outcome will be a nightmare of 'Brazilianization': vastly unequal societies scarred by crime and delinquency, in which everyone including the privileged and affluent is subject to close monitoring and surveillance. Community, civil society and the welfare state all collapse, while the natural environment is relentlessly degraded. The reality of free world trade will not be prosperity for all; social polarization within societies will be replicated in the relations between them.

Some ostensible challenges to globalization are, for Beck, no such thing; appearances to the contrary, they depend upon globalism and offer no prospect of salvation from it. They are various forms of protectionism, a negative globalism. *Conservative protectionists* idolize the nation-state; only in a national heartland can the values of family, religion and community be rooted. Yet they also champion the neoliberal dynamic, including the drive towards a world market that systematically undermines these selfsame values. *Green protectionists* are, according to Beck, curiously wedded to the nation-state, despite the obvious need to tackle ecological problems globally. Their entrenched hostility to modernity limits their effectiveness as a bulwark against globalism. Beck's argument seems rather dated: there is nothing inherently ethnocentric in green politics, and green activists have been striving to create alliances across national and continental boundaries. *Red protectionists* are living in the socialist past – a utopia that has been decisively rejected. Since none of these protectionist responses have come to terms with the realities of globality and globalization, they cannot halt the onward march of globalism. They are political dead ends.

A crucial element in Beck's critique of globalism is the claim that it induces political paralysis. Although the transition to globality brings a transformation in the social, political and cultural order, and requires a paradigm shift in our social theorizing, none of this entails the collapse of political agency. The 'thought-virus' of globalism tries to infect us with the notion that nothing can be done to halt or deflect the automatic workings of the world market. A deadly fatalism lies at the heart of cultural pessimism, and can take the sting out of apparently powerful critiques of the market – as we shall see in the discussion of George Ritzer's work on McDonaldization and globalization.

The Globalization of Nothing?

Ritzer's *The Globalization of Nothing* (2004) carries further the analysis he advanced in *The McDonaldization of Society* (1996). The burden of the argument is contained in his concept of nothing, which he defines as follows: 'generally centrally conceived and controlled social forms that are comparatively devoid of distinctive substantive content' (2004: xi). Nothing is sub-divided into four types: non-places such as shopping malls and casinos, non-things such as branded clothing, non-people such as workers in fast-food outlets or call centres, and non-services such as self-service using ATM machines or the Internet.

Nothing, according to Ritzer, is being globalized; but there is a fundamental conflict within globalization. On the one hand there is the process identified by Roland Robertson as *glocalization*, through which the global and the local interact to produce new products, services and social forms. On the other hand there is what Ritzer calls *grobalization* – a deliberately ugly word for a sinister process. Fuelled by the imperialistic ambitions of nation-states and capitalist corporations, grobalization tends to obliterate the local and impose the global. Normally, what it imposes is, in Ritzer's terminology, forms of nothing.

Between them, glocalization and grobalization have reduced the purely local almost to the point of oblivion. If we accept that Ritzer is right about this, we are left with four viable social forms. The *grobal nothing* is exemplified by the Disney Corporation: a non-place (such as a Disney theme park) staffed by non-persons (cast members), stocked with non-things (Mouse-ear hats) and offering non-service (queuing for attractions). At the opposite pole stands the *glocal something*: a place (such as a craft barn) staffed by persons (craftspersons), stocked with things (local crafts) and offering a service (a demonstration). Ritzer argues that the grobal tends to go with nothing, and the glocal with something; in Weberian terms, there is an elective affinity between them. He also asserts that there is an overpowering trend, accelerated by the victory of capitalism over communism, towards the triumph of grobal nothing.

Inspection of the remaining two categories, the grobal something and the glocal nothing, is more revealing than

Ritzer seems to realize. As an example of the *grobal something* he gives a place (such as a museum) staffed by persons (knowledgeable guides), stocked with things (a touring art exhibition) and offering a service (a guided tour of the exhibition). Here, by contrast, is a *glocal nothing*: a non-place (such as a souvenir shop) staffed by non-persons (souvenir shop clerks), stocked with non-things (tourist trinkets) and offering non-service (self-service). These illustrations demonstrate clearly, I would argue, that in the terms of Ritzer's argument what is decisive is the distinction between something and nothing; his grobal–glocal dimension is far less important. Consider his example of the glocal nothing, the souvenir shop: what transformation, what new social form, has the glocal brought about? They may be locally produced, but the goods are mere trinkets; the staff are not required to possess skills or knowledge, and they provide little real service other than taking customers' money. In this example, the trinkets remain trinkets; nothing has not been turned into something. Now consider his example of the grobal something, a museum housing a touring exhibition of great paintings. Here, the works on display are great art, the guides are well-informed professionals, and the service they offer, a guided tour, adds genuine value to the experience. In this case, the grobal has not ruined the paintings; the van Goghs, in Ritzer's example, have not been transmuted from something to nothing. Settings such as this are not so much grobal as *cosmopolitan*.

Ritzer's definition of nothing bears little resemblance to other work on the concept. He rapidly reviews a range of theorists, from the Greek philosophers Parmenides and Zeno to Kant, Hegel, Heidegger and Sartre. Their work, it transpires, has little relevance to Ritzer's thesis. Among the sociologists, only Marx and Simmel are mentioned. Marx is said not to be relevant, since the concept of nothing is judged to be too abstract and philosophical for a revolutionary materialist (Ritzer 2004: 191). Of all the writers surveyed, only Simmel is seen as working on nothing as conceptualized here. Ritzer refers approvingly to Simmel's pessimistic analysis of 'the tragedy of culture': that people are increasingly alienated from an 'objective culture' which they can neither comprehend nor control. For Simmel, this was a latent problem in all cultures; Ritzer turns it into the problem of the meaninglessness of nothing.

A fault-line runs through *The Globalization of Nothing*: is it value-free analysis or cultural critique? Ritzer claims the former, though he also appears to want it both ways. He argues that although his concept of nothing may sound like a criticism, 'forms that are largely empty of social content are *not necessarily problematic*' (Ritzer 2004: xi). He also denies that his own 'preference' for something has any greater weight than personal taste and sensibility, acknowledges that he is vulnerable to the charge of being 'elitist', and refuses to condemn anyone who embraces nothing wholeheartedly. He made similar points in apparent defence of McDonaldization in his earlier work.

Notwithstanding his disclaimers, the thrust of the book is clearly a cultural critique. The very definition of nothing as 'comparatively devoid of distinctive substantive content' gives an unmistakable clue to the standing of nothing. Nothing is not Zen, or self-denial, or aesthetic minimalism, or the *via negativa*, the 'negative way' of approaching God by rejecting the idolatrous 'content' of human attempts to comprehend the divine. Attempts to turn nothing into something – whether by the manufacturers and retailers of nothing, who seek ways of re-enchanting a disenchanted world, or by consumers who try to inject a subjective meaning into what is objectively nothing – are doomed to failure.

At the end of the book, Ritzer says that we must make up our own mind about nothing. Even so, he offers more than a hint of the correct answer. Although he will not call the lovers of nothing 'judgmental dopes', he hopes that 'if everyone gave as much time and thought to the issues discussed in this book as has the author, they too would be concerned about the long-term trend in the direction of nothing and the loss associated with it' (Ritzer 2004: 216). Earlier he has said that something requires 'far more sophisticated tastes than nothing' (2004: 100).

The book is, manifestly, a sustained defence of something against nothing. Just as he analysed 'the irrationality of rationality' in his critique of McDonaldization, so here he underlines that the fundamental irrationality of the contemporary world is 'the increasing loss of something amid monumental abundance' (2004: 201). People labouring in Third World sweatshops suffer a 'double affliction'; they produce most of the world's nothings but cannot afford them. Globalization sweeps away the local, from which most cultural innovation springs. Fast-food restaurants displace the 'great good places' celebrated by Ray Oldenburg (1997) – those public, third places apart from home and work, where passers-by and a regular clientele meet for convivial conversation. The great good place is a building block of civil society; the fast-food restaurant is a pit stop for refuelling.

What arguments does Ritzer give in support of his claim that nothing is not necessarily problematic? I suggest he makes five main points. Nothings are often convenient; nothings may be cheap; nothings may be efficient; nothings are abundant; and, conversely, somethings can be poor quality. Upon examination, these arguments are scarcely an overwhelming endorsement of nothing. Nothings are perhaps convenient, cheap and efficient. But convenience is a rather thin virtue, and may be little more than a justification of laziness. Low price is all too often an illusion, as is efficiency (as Ritzer argued powerfully in his critique of McDonaldization). Nothings are abundant; but we have already seen Ritzer's verdict, that the abundance of nothing is the fundamental irrationality of our times. Finally, something can indeed be disappointing; the 'distinctive content' offered by Ritzer's favoured example, a greasy spoon café, may be disgusting. Avoiding disappointment could, however, only be guaranteed in a risk-free monoculture of grobal nothings. The possibility of disappointment is a necessary condition of a truly enjoyable meal.

Ritzer's critique of nothing raises the question, can something be preserved? Exactly the same issue arose in relation to McDonaldization: can it be resisted? In both cases, Ritzer's attitude is despairing; he declares himself a Weberian cultural pessimist. His discussion of resistance to McDonaldization presents a list of possibilities that include the tongue-in cheek and the impractical. Significantly, he discusses individual escape bids, not collective forms of resistance. The plucky few may escape, but the prison remains intact. Escape from McDonaldization is presented as doubly improbable, first because there is almost nowhere to go, and second because few people want to escape anyway. McDonaldization has penetrated our consciousness, moulding our tastes to make us satisfied with the goods and services it delivers.

The grobalization of nothing is similarly argued to be all-conquering. Genuinely local goods and services have been virtually wiped out (Ritzer 2004: 109–10); the best we can expect to find are glocal somethings. In so far as cultural innovation is possible, it will arise from the interplay of glocal somethings; it can no longer be local in character. Unfortunately, there is a depressing trend for glocal somethings to be supplanted by glocal nothings, as producers struggle to meet growing demand for their products. Once capitalist corporations scent the opportunity to make easy profits, glocal nothings are fated to become grobal.

If McDonald's is the totem of McDonaldization, Disney theme parks with their 'outrageous inauthenticity' (Ritzer 2004: 129) are icons of the grobalization of nothing. Disney's manipulation of culture is a spectacular achievement. It blends sentimentality toward the past, enjoyment of the present and optimism for the future, all suffused with the warmth of family relationships. If Disney engulfs time past, time present and time future, resistance is scarcely conceivable.

Ritzer's analysis of McDonaldization and the grobalization of nothing is, I have argued, not a dispassionate commentary but a searing cultural critique. As such, it may backfire. If these forces are irresistible, what would be the point of resistance, other than as an artistic gesture? A feature of such corporations is precisely that they offer their delicacies as irresistible; irresistibility connotes not imperialism but seduction. Far from posing a challenge, cultural pessimism may be the ultimate capitulation to global capitalism and the 'free' market.

Market Socialism

Market socialism is largely a product of the twentieth century. Its first major incarnation was in the so-called 'socialist calculation debate' of the 1920s. The Polish economist Oskar Lange argued, against the Austrian economists' critiques of socialism, that rational planning is achievable under state socialism. Central planners can simulate the market price mechanism: through a process of trial and error they can set and adjust prices to reflect the interplay of supply and demand. The centrally planned economy, on Lange's account, can succeed in allocating resources efficiently.

The socialist calculation debate revolved around economic efficiency, not democracy, or liberty, or workers' rights, or equality (Pierson 1995: 83). Lacking these crucial aspects, it did not reflect the preoccupations of Western socialists. Nor did it address all the problems of socialism as identified by the Austrian advocates of the free market: low motivation, lack of innovation, suppression of entrepreneurship, and failure to mobilize the wealth of tacit knowledge diffused throughout society.

During the Second World War and the ensuing Cold War, market socialism fell out of favour. Interest in its ideals and programme was rekindled in the 1970s and 1980s. Reformers saw it as a vehicle for rejuvenating the failing economies and moribund political cultures of state socialism. In the capitalist West, some on the Left thought of it as a way of avoiding the problems both of traditional socialism and of welfarist social democracy. They believed it not only offered a theoretical path out of these problems, but also had the potential to appeal to a wide electorate. Its feasibility as an electoral and a political programme was proclaimed a cardinal virtue.

On the face of it, socialism and the market appear to be incompatible. Markets connote capitalism, private property and consumer sovereignty, whereas socialism demands collective ownership and control of economic resources. In practice, however, socialism has always relied upon selective use of markets, even in the Soviet Union. Conversely, one might add, capitalism has invariably depended upon a degree of planning by central authorities. Even at the height of the Cold War, practice on both sides of the Iron Curtain was far more mixed than pure theories might suggest. Market socialism is less single-minded than neoliberalism or traditional socialism; its proposals are pragmatic and pluralistic. Reconciling socialism and the market may be judged difficult, but that does not mean it is an incoherent project.

Market socialists aim to disentangle the market and capitalism, so as to reclaim for socialism the most beneficial features of the market. Frankly acknowledging the proven problems both of state socialism and social democracy, market socialists try to hold fast to socialism's core values and principles. Goods, services and labour will be distributed by the market, but in the context of collective ownership of the means of production. The goal is to enjoy the fruits of the market system without the blight of capitalism.

Miller (1989: 9–10) and Pierson (1995: 86–95) specify four key objectives of market socialism. First, to use the market mechanism in order to achieve efficient production of goods and services. The problem is to achieve this without replicating the extreme inequalities of capitalism. Second, to pursue genuine democracy, curbing the role of state and contesting the power of commercial firms. Third, to protect and enhance workers' rights and liberties, given that the capitalist market promises freedoms but offers only semblances, such as formal freedom of contract between highly unequal parties. Fourth, to achieve social justice, and in particular far greater equality in income distribution. A programme that values efficiency, democracy, freedom and equality would enjoy wide popularity, Miller contends, since it 'matches the aspirations of our age' (Miller 1989: 4).

Pierson adds a fifth consideration to these goals. In the eyes of many market socialists, there is no alternative. Traditional socialism has been discredited, not least but not only because of the terrible example of communism. Marxian analysis is terminally flawed: the labour theory of value is false, capitalism is not anarchy, socialism cannot abolish scarcity, and the industrial proletariat, a diminishing force, has neither the capacity nor the will to overthrow capitalism. Social democracy is not the answer: the so-called social democratic consensus has been shattered, Keynesian political economy led ultimately to crisis, and the welfare state is unsustainable. Embracing the market is the only viable way to contest capitalism. To many market socialists, what this means is not a joyous but a reluctant acceptance of the market. Emphasis on realism, pragmatism and feasibility has been at the heart of most advocacy of market socialism.

Unsurprisingly, market socialism has come under fire from both Right and Left, the commonest criticism being that it is a contradiction in terms. To free marketeers, it cannot honour its promise to reconcile the market and socialism. Market socialists may profess that they want to curb the state; even so, they do not and cannot embrace the radically minimal state favoured by most free marketeers. That being so, market socialists are not able to give to the market the absolute pre-eminence that free marketeers demand. Pierson (1995: 213) puts it sharply: 'For the most committed neo-liberals, the very best social order is one which guarantees the integrity of market-like exchanges between freely-contracting individuals, *irrespective of particular substantive outcomes*.' Yet a central objective of market socialism is precisely to eliminate the gross disparities of wealth, prestige and power that inevitably follow from the free play of market forces. Such an aim requires radical intervention of the kind abhorrent to advocates of the free market.

As for the critique from the Left, Callinicos speaks for many in arguing that a market socialist system would be permanently at risk of lapsing back into capitalism unless it were subject to such stringent controls that it would no longer warrant the label *market* socialism (Callinicos 2003: 119). Markets cannot be reconciled to socialism: they are fundamentally undemocratic, their freedoms are spurious for all but the rich, and they inevitably lead to gross inequality and injustice. And, despite their pretensions to the contrary, the persistence of market failures demonstrates that they are not even efficient.

To be identified as a contradiction in terms would be devastating enough. Pierson delivers a further blow by attacking market socialism precisely at the point where it ought to be strongest. A defining claim made on behalf of market socialism is that it is feasible. Unlike traditional socialism it is, so it claims, realistic and pragmatic. It may fall short of the theoretical ideal of full-blooded socialism, but that ideal is an unattainable utopia. Market socialism may be second best, as many of its advocates concede, but it is still vastly preferable to the capitalist alternative.

When, however, we examine this claim for market social ism, it turns out that feasibility is equated with logical consistency and theoretical coherence. That was a characteristic of the earlier socialist calculation debate: what mattered was to demonstrate that socialist planning could in principle be rational. But even if market socialism is coherent theoretically, that by itself does not make it a realizable political

programme. How many electors will vote for market socialism, and how will it be implemented if the majority do vote
for it?

Pierson identifies two core problems of feasibility (1995:
208–11). First, if market socialism is to commend itself to the
electorate, it needs a plausible programme of transition that
appeals to a wide range of interests and does not depend upon
violent disruptions. Its programme must be presented as grad-
ualist, but it implies huge upheavals. The dilemma is arguably
unresolvable: to command popular support, market socialism
must promise gradual reform, but to be a feasible programme
it requires a fundamental reordering of state and society.

Second, market socialism presents itself as a programme of
reform within the nation-state, not as a strategy of global
restructuring. The failure to address globalization has proved
a grave weakness. More than anything else, it accounts for the
impression that market socialism is not tomorrow's project
but yesterday's dream. And yet, as Pierson also remarks
(1995: 217), 'So long as it makes sense to study capitalist
forms and relations, and to consider alternatives to these,
there is value in thinking in socialist terms.'

The Third Way

'The overall aim of third way politics should be to help
citizens pilot their way through the major revolutions of our
time: globalization, transformations in personal life, and our
relationship to nature' (Giddens 1998: 64). This quotation
from Anthony Giddens's first book-length exposition of the
Third Way shows the scope of what is envisaged.

One might argue that market socialism failed adequately to
address any of these three dimensions. Giddens, Held and
other leading analysts of the Third Way have little to say about
market socialism, or indeed any form of socialism, for the
simple reason that they believe it is no longer credible. For
them, the significant ideological opponent is not socialism but
neoliberalism.

In a passage trenchantly entitled 'the death of socialism',
Giddens enumerates the reasons for its demise (1998: 3–8). At
root, the Marxian hope that socialist societies would unleash

the capacity locked up in capitalism, generating greater wealth and spreading it more equally throughout society, has proved an illusion. Capitalism, not socialism, was economically dynamic; by the 1970s, it was becoming clear that state social-ism was stagnant beyond recovery. In Western Europe, where socialism took the form of classical social democracy, it too came under severe strain in the 1970s; its inherent prob-lems lent plausibility to the neoliberal agenda of the radical Right. Classical social democracy could not deliver its promise to manage the mixed economy so as to generate economic growth, secure a harmonious social contract between trade unions and employers, provide full employment, and sustain a welfare state that offered to all citizens first-class cradle-to-grave provision free at the point of delivery. It failed to come to grips with social and cultural changes that were trans-forming the world. As we saw in the quotation from Giddens at the beginning of this section, these changes were threefold. Social democracy failed to see the significance of globaliza-tion; it relied upon sovereign nation-states co-operating inter-nationally but without any significant changes to global structures of governance. It failed to confront fundamental shifts in civil society: deindustrialization and the decline of intergenerationally stable working-class communities, the erosion of traditional class and political alignments, the dis-placement of the male 'breadwinner' as women participated more fully in paid employment, the challenges of a multicul-tural society, the significance of 'identity politics' and the rise of consumerism. It was, finally, slow to meet the challenge of environmental concerns; for too long the green agenda was seen as a distraction from real politics.

This account of the problems of classic social democracy would appear more applicable to the UK experience than to that of the Nordic countries, a point not lost on Giddens's critics. In response, he draws attention to social and economic problems in those countries (Giddens 2000: 16–17, 98–100), in particular Sweden, though he tends to play down their achievements in combating social inequality and fostering their citizens' stock of social capital.

Giddens's objective is to renew centre-left social democracy. The programme he outlines (Giddens 1998) calls for democ-ratization of the apparatus of the state, including devolution of power from the centre to regional and local authorities; an active civil society and a vigorous voluntary sector; effective policing with the consent and involvement of local communities; and support for what he calls 'the democratic family', which is based on reciprocal rights and responsibilities among all the parties. In some considerable measure, this programme is designed to recapture the core values of civilized society that have been appropriated by the Right, including the principles governing market relationships.

Even though 'the neoliberal idea that markets should almost everywhere stand in place of public goods is ridiculous', social democrats 'need to overcome some of their worries and fears about markets' (Giddens 2000: 32). To do so means, above all, to confront the challenge of globalization. I would argue that there are three key elements in this. Second-wave social democrats need to recognize globalization as more than an economic trend. They must also demonstrate that globalization can be regulated effectively. First, however, they need to establish that globalization is a reality and not hyperbole – or, as critics have begun to call it, globaloney.

Globalization, as Held et al. put it (1999: 2), entails 'the widening, deepening and speeding up of worldwide interconnectedness in all aspects of contemporary life, from the cultural to the criminal, the financial to the spiritual'. It has four dimensions: *extensity*, which refers to the geographic spread of social, political and economic activities across national frontiers; *intensity*, that is the magnitude of interconnectedness of such activities; *velocity*, or the speed of global interactions and flows; and *impact*, which includes its effect on policies, institutions, the distribution of wealth and power, and the structuring of fundamental relations between state, social institutions and civil society. Deploying these dimensions, Held et al. seek to show that, although it has historical precursors, contemporary globalization is a totally new phenomenon.

Contemporary globalization is described as 'thick', scoring highly on all four dimensions. At the opposite pole is 'thin globalization', historical examples being the silk and luxury trade circuits that linked Europe with East Asia. Intensity, velocity and impact were all low. Only extensity was high, but that is a minimal condition of globalization. This thin type of globalization is a possible future, if protectionism takes hold.

Two intermediate types are identified. Expansive globalization corresponds to the age of European imperialism. Critics sometimes point to this era as evidence that globalization is nothing new. The old empires did indeed have a wide geographic reach and a huge impact on colonial peoples, but their velocity and interconnectedness were low.

Diffused globalization scores highly on all dimensions apart from the one that really counts: impact. Those who accept the reality of globalization but not its far-reaching consequences tend to argue for this type of globalization, since it preserves wide freedom of manoeuvre for individual nation-states. Such an approach characterizes those who prefer a 'Europe of nations' to a 'European superstate'.

Based on their analysis of the four dimensions, Held et al. reject the claims of those theorists, whom they call 'hyper-globalizers', who advance the radical claim that the nation-state is effectively impotent. They also reject the claims of the 'sceptics', for whom internationalization – increased interactions between national economies – is a reality, whereas globalization is a myth.

Hyperglobalizers and sceptics have one thing in common: the first see globalization as an economic phenomenon, the second as an economic myth. Neoliberalism celebrates economic globalization, since it means a further expansion of the market system. Neoliberals see opportunities for all societies to prosper, provided that they exploit their competitive advantage. Protectionism is not a viable option; success will come to societies that manage globalization effectively.

For Marxists, the target is global capitalism. Callinicos insists that 'the anti-globalization movement' is absurdly inappropriate term for a movement that revels in its own international character and that has successfully mobilized support across all five continents. Better, he says, to give it its true name: the anti-capitalist movement (Callinicos 2003: 13–16). This point becomes the first of his nine anti capitalist theses (Callinicos 2001: 111–20): the enemy is not globalization, but global capitalism. This implies, contrary to Giddens and Held, that globalization is primarily economic. Callinicos's second thesis emphasizes the point: the core institutions of global capitalism are the multinational corporations, the leading capitalist states and the international institutions that reflect their

interests. The ninth and last thesis is unequivocal: transcend-
ing capitalism requires a revolutionary transformation of
society.

Given this, it is unsurprising that Callinicos's verdict on
the Third Way is unfavourable; it means 'the abandonment of
any challenge to global capitalism' (Callinicos 2001: viii). Its
critique of neoliberalism is feeble; in seeking to accommodate
the market it unwittingly supplies neoliberalism with an ideological gloss; in Touraine's words, it is 'a form of neoliberalism
tempered by social policies' (2001: 91). What it allegedly fails
to do is challenge the 'fetish' of economic growth to which
both neoliberals and socialists are devoted (Hamilton, C.
2004). The Third Way's commitment to environmentalism is
uncertain; it features as well-intentioned aspirations to sustainable development.

These critics argue that the Third Way seeks to adapt the
state to the market, not vice versa. Neoliberalism is not, in any
case, the real enemy. That position is occupied by the capitalist
mode of production. The revamped social democratic project
is to control global capitalism by strengthening international
regulatory institutions. But these – the G7, the World Bank, the
World Trade Organization, NATO, the European Union – are
agents of capitalism, not the means to hold it in check. Their
agenda is neither environmentalism nor social democracy, but
the Washington Consensus.

The critiques launched by Touraine and Callinicos are
typical, not least in coming from the Left. Right-wing commentators have had far less to say about the Third Way, which
may show that it poses no real challenge to right-wing thought
and practice. Whatever the case, the reception of the Third
Way demonstrates that overcoming the polarization between
pro- and anti-market thought is not easy. Whether it is our
truest friend or our most implacable enemy, the market is seen
by Right, Left and Centre as a dominant force in the contemporary world.

I pointed out earlier that there are three key elements in the
case for second-wave social democracy. So far we have encoun-
tered two: that contemporary globalization is a fundamentally
new phenomenon, and that it can be controlled by international regulatory bodies. The third element is the claim that
globalization is more than a purely economic phenomenon.

Giddens has always insisted on this point, while Held puts it at the centre of his *Global Covenant*. Tomlinson asserts at the very beginning of his *Globalization and Culture* (1999: 1): 'Globalization lies at the heart of modern culture; cultural practices lie at the heart of globalization.' Globalization is not and never has been simply an economic matter. Held dismisses the agenda of the Washington Consensus not only as unattractive but as narrowly economic: selling public assets to the private sector, deregulating the economy, and cutting taxes and government expenditure on welfare and social programmes (see chapter 2, pp. 49–56). The revitalized social democratic agenda, in contrast, depends upon cultural transformation and sweeping reforms of social institutions. It is committed to cosmopolitan ethical ideals which it seeks to embody in social, political and economic institutions which are necessarily global in scope. 'At its centre is the requirement that legitimate political authority, at all levels, must uphold, and be delimited by, a commitment to the values and principles which underpin political equality, democratic politics, human rights, political and social justice, and the sound stewardship of the environment' (Held 2004: 162).

These ideals may be cosmopolitan, but does that make them universal? Held turns to this question at the end of *Global Covenant*. He argues that the values are not simply 'Western', even if some of them first emerged in the course of the eighteenth-century Enlightenment. The principles he sets out are 'the foundation of a fair, humane and decent society, of whatever religion or cultural tradition' (Held 2004: 176); grounded in the moral status of every human being, they are the building blocks of freedom and equality. They imply a form of democracy, but democracy is not a purely Western invention or reality; on the contrary, it predominates in the Third World. If size matters, then it is not the United States, whose population stands at some 290 million, but India, with a population of over a billion, that is the world's largest democracy.

The question remains, what of fundamentalist religions that reject democratic values in the name of a transcendent god who has decreed otherwise? Not everyone sees democracy as the benign alternative to totalitarianism. For some, democracy, the rule of the people, is an evil alternative to theocracy, the rule of God (or God's servants). Held does not shirk this problem, nor does he avoid what is probably the most pressing and complex case of all: Islam. Held's answer is to turn the problem back to the social settings from which it arises. All the great world religions contain diverse bodies of thought and practice. Fundamentalism is a problem not just for the West, but for everyone who values autonomy, rights and justice. Although it does not imply the privileging of any religious tradition, or indeed the privileging of religion over secularity, it seems hard to avoid the conclusion that social democracy necessarily stands opposed to all forms of fundamentalism, not least the fundamentalism of the market.

In Defence of Practices

In *After Virtue*, Alasdair MacIntyre introduces the concept of the 'practice', which he defines as follows:

> any coherent and complex form of socially established co-operative human activity through which goods internal to that form of activity are realised in the course of trying to achieve those standards of excellence which are appropriate to, and partially definitive of, that form of activity, with the result that human powers to achieve excellence, and human conceptions of the ends and goods involved, are systematically extended. (MacIntyre 1981: 175)

This concept of practice has been taken up in a series of publications by Russell Keat (1991; 1994; 2000).

Goods that are internal to a practice can be specified only by reference to the distinctive nature of that practice; for example, the *elegance* of a mathematical proof, the *dynamism* of a move in chess or the *critical analysis* displayed in a student's essay. We learn the meaning of these normative criteria by participating in the practice and subjecting our performances to evaluations by experienced practitioners. To outsiders the criteria are often obscure and sometimes meaningless, which is why beginners have to learn them. The character of an external good, in contrast, is not dependent upon the particular nature of the practice through which it may be achieved. External goods are incidental benefits of the performance of a practice. Prime examples of external goods are money, power and prestige.

Practices require institutions for their long-term viability. Chess and sociology are practices, chess clubs and universities are institutional carriers of those practices. Just as we can contrast internal and external goods, so, following Weber (1964/1922), we can distinguish between autonomous institutions, whose constitution and practices have been established by their own members acting on their own authority, and heteronomous institutions, where they have been imposed from outside.

Institutions are, inescapably, authority structures. In the most elevated examples, autonomous institutions uphold standards of excellence that typically have been cultivated for centuries. Among the virtues they demand, therefore, is a willingness on the part of novices to submit their work to the judgement of legitimate authorities. Joining a practice is tantamount to entering an apprenticeship. There must be a willingness to learn, and to accept, at least initially, the criteria that prevail within that practice; so, for example, students of sociology are not permitted to challenge the desirability of critical analysis, nor to espouse the advantages of plagiarism. What is sought is 'not an attitude of deference or passivity, but of (potentially critical) respect' (Keat 1994: 37).

As Keat observes, people who work in non-market cultural institutions typically see the market as a threat. Their claim is that to introduce market forces into the practice would be to compromise its integrity, distort its character and divert it from its true mission. The market, on this view, will substitute external goods for internal ones; excellence will be subverted by commercialism. Some practitioners, seduced by lust for money, power and prestige, will 'sell out' their principles, provoking accusations by their colleagues of betrayal, of a *trahison des clercs*.

Despite this, it is mistake to see the distinction between external and internal goods as implying a clash between egoistic and altruistic motivations. Keat's argument does not require practitioners to be altruists. Practitioners can have a mixture of motives such as enjoyment of the cultural practice or belief in its capacity to enhance human life. Unless they have private means they also need to make a living. They may even recognize that the practice is not viable unless it is supported by a clientele and an institution; no students, no university, no sociological practice. Institutions are bound to be concerned not only with internal criteria of excellence but also with the external goods of money, prestige and power. Clients, like practitioners, may be expected to have mixed motives; the point, says Keat, is that these should not jeopardize the internal goods that define the practice and give it its meaning.

An obvious problem with the defence of practices is the charge of elitism. Keat is quick to point out that he is not privileging high culture; defending practices 'is just as much concerned with the market's threat to soap opera as to classical opera' (Keat 2000: 7). He also distinguishes two aspects of elitism, rejecting elitism of access (classical music is only for the discerning few) but upholding elitism of judgement (classical music must be evaluated primarily by its own distinguished practitioners, the composers, performers and musicologists). Elitism of judgement does not imply elitism of access; many practitioners deplore the social exclusiveness and sheer snobbery that can mar classical music or, for that matter, ancient universities. It seems clear that resistance to the market need not involve commitment to elitism of access. The problem of elitism was a major concern for Bourdieu, who sought, as Lane comments (2000: 184), 'to reconcile a critique of the arbitrary and elitist nature of autonomous fields and their products with a defence of that autonomy against the incursions of the market'.

Critics who argue that the way to counter elitism is to subject practices to the free play of market forces usually appeal to the principle of consumer sovereignty. Consumers are assumed to know what their preferences are and whether they have been satisfied by a particular supplier; these two things are, in fact, all they need to know. They have direct, first-hand access to their own wants; such knowledge is incontestable. Consumer sovereignty is radically subjectivist; moral, aesthetic and political questions are matters of personal preference, and have no objective or authoritative answers. There is, as Keat says (1991: 227), 'a kind of natural alliance between value-subjectivism and the market'; thus in economic analysis consumers' wants are taken as given. This subjectivism is precisely what concerns the guardians of practices. For if there are no objective ways of judging the value of cultural practices, then the obvious and justifiable thing to do is to assess them not by the arbitrary self-serving judgements of their producers but by aggregating the preferences of consumers.

In response, Keat argues that cultural practices are justified not by the satisfaction of consumers but by the well-being of audiences, where well-being is a product of autonomy (as discussed above in chapter 3, pp. 109–10). The consumer, as Bauman argues, may be seduced, whereas the autonomous person is critical and reflective, and will measure the import-ance of consumer satisfaction in relation to other projects in life, such as the cultivation of friendships, participation in political and moral causes, or the pursuit of learning. The place of consumption in people's lives is not itself a matter of consumer preference.

Even if such a defence of cultural practices against market forces stands up, there is another line of attack that needs to be countered. What if institutions become moribund and practitioners complacent and reactionary? The authority vested in cultural practitioners can easily degenerate into self-satisfaction and inertia. In the professions, it can lead to con-tempt for the clients the practitioner is supposed to serve. In the sciences, it can mean an undue reliance on outdated para-digms and procedures, so that a proper openness to new dis-coveries is supplanted by a dogmatic scientism that treats yesterday's provisional findings as eternal truths. In the arts, it may mean academicism: the cultivation of formal technique and worship of sterile conventions at the expense of innova-tion and creativity.

What this argument misses is the diversity that exists within cultural practices, and the potential for rebellion against authority when it becomes hidebound. Cultural prac-tices are typically pluralistic, and divided into rival 'schools'; novices are able to exercise choice at the point of entry. Nor should it be forgotten that the prospect of innovation is one of the exciting features of cultural practices, and is an ambi-tion that a significant minority of new entrants may cherish. Iconoclastic manifestos, radical new perspectives and scien-tific paradigm-shifts recurrently disturb the orthodoxies of academically approved art and 'normal' science (Kuhn 1962).

The possibility of revolt against a given authority is an engine of innovation; it is not the same thing as subjectivist rejection of all authority.

In subsequent work, Keat expresses concern that his earlier defence of cultural practices and institutions against the threat of the market was based on a questionable assumption. The problem was that he appeared to be taking at face value the way that neoclassical economics represents 'the market' (Keat 2000: 11). He is now inclined to argue, first, that the market system is not necessarily incompatible with the integrity of practices, and second, that markets can deliver worthwhile benefits to consumers. Unless we fall into the elitist trap of discounting consumer tastes as in some sense degenerate, we have to take seriously the argument that practices can be of more benefit to their practitioners than their clients.

Keat's reformulation is in line with a core thesis of this book: the market is a deeply problematic construct. It is not 'the market' that endangers cultural practices in the West, but the economic demands of capitalist corporations and the political programme of neoliberal governments seeking to marketize all social relations. This programme, as Keat says, aims at de-differentiation: all social institutions are to become profit-maximizing businesses, everyone must become an entrepreneur, and everything must have a price.

Bourdieu's work on the changing power structures in France bears witness to the ascendancy of neoliberal ideology and practices in a setting that has hitherto been resistant to them. In *Distinction*, Bourdieu documents a shift away from cultural capital towards economic capital as the key determinant of lifestyles among the middle classes. It is accompanied by more individualistic values, and the rise of the new conservatism as the dominant ideology. Within multinational corporations, power has been transferred away from scientists and engineers towards technocrats and experts in corporate finance. In the field of higher education (Bourdieu 1996), the once supreme École Normale Supérieure, whose curriculum continues to enjoy academic independence from the demands of the world of business, has lost status and influence compared to the more business-oriented Sciences Po, and the École des Hautes Études Commerciales. Even the École Nationale d'Administration, which trains France's elite civil servants, has watered down its public service ethos and become increasingly technocratic. (The ENA's fall from grace is underlined by its being obliged to quit Paris in 2005 and relocate to Strasbourg.) As Lane points out, graduates of more technocratic and managerialist *grandes écoles* are increasingly assuming positions of power in state administration as well as private business. France has not adopted Anglo-Saxon neoliberalism wholesale, but given it a French inflection: 'France's ruling elite' as Lane observes (2000: 170), 'has thus not so much abandoned all faith in state intervention, as reinterpreted the discourse, goals and methods of neo-liberalism through the medium of a peculiarly French tradition of centralised state planning or *dirigisme*.' One cost has been a marked loss of academic autonomy by the country's most prestigious university institutions.

Recognizing the problem of reifying 'the market' leads to a reconsideration of the relationship between internal and external goods. I said earlier, following MacIntyre and Keat, that internal goods are often unclear and occasionally incomprehensible to outsiders. Why should a mathematical proof be elegant, and what is elegance anyway? Surely the most important thing is that the proof is valid? The answer is that elegance can only be fully understood and appreciated through open-minded participation in the practice by novices who are willing to learn from their seniors.

By implication, external goods such as money, prestige and power are radically different from this. External goods are not puzzling. We know only too well that they are valuable, and do not need to learn to appreciate them. *Surely, though, this is not true?* External goods are not unproblematic universals. As Keat recognizes, we often have to learn to put a price on things, and frequently refuse to do so. Similarly, we have to learn to become ambitious for prestige and power; they do not come naturally to everyone. The value of external goods, like that of internal goods, is socially constructed.

Neoliberal claims that marketization is the way to inject dynamism and diversity into cultural practices are poorly supported by the evidence. Paradoxically, market-based solutions typically create cumbersome bureaucracies and mechanisms of control. Quantification of outputs and their aggregation into league tables serves promotional culture at least as much as it benefits the public. Whether marketization is a means to promote innovation and diversity is open to doubt.

Promotional Culture: The Case of Universities

Promotional culture is defined by Andrew Wernick as 'a functionally interdependent complex within which the line between what is incidental as advertising and what is ostensibly its primary content, as information and entertainment, is reduced at most to a matter of level and degree' (Wernick 1991: 100). Postmodernists have emphasized the collapse of firm distinctions between such categories as fact and value, reality and appearance, fact and fiction. This, says Wernick, should not be a cause for rejoicing.

If the development of capitalism brought about the ascendancy within signifying practices of the promotional mode and the commodity form, the fall of communism ushered in their global hegemony. The outcome is that other practices and institutions have been overwhelmed by promotionalism; 'the range of cultural phenomena which, at least as one of their functions, serve to communicate a promotional message has become, today, virtually co-extensive with our produced symbolic world' (Wernick 1991: 182). This culture, a dense communicative complex, has become culturally pervasive. Promotional culture is one of the most potent ways in which the market threatens to colonize other domains. Among those domains is education, including higher education.

Drawing mainly on the North American experience, Wernick argues that universities have become ever more deeply entangled in competitive, promotional culture. It is not just a question of clever advertising. 'What really matters', he contends, 'is all the accumulated promotional capital that has gone into constructing a school's perceived academic reputation' (Wernick 1991: 161). Student recruitment, students' academic qualifications, academic publishing and academic careers are all caught up in the promotional vortex. Take student recruitment, for instance. There is far more to this than simply attracting enough students to fill the available places. Students are not just customers, they are property, a bankable asset. The higher the quality of the student intake (as measured

by competitive examinations), the more prestige is accorded to
the university. In the UK, students' grades in the school-leaving
A-level examination are a major factor in the league tables of
university performance published in the quality press and
widely disseminated in schools. Reference to these league
tables is regularly made in universities' promotional material.
The higher the university's reputation, the greater the
exchange-value of its degrees – a point not lost on students.
The higher the university's reputation, the greater the career
prospects of its staff – a point not lost on academics. The
higher the university's reputation, the greater its attraction to
potential donors – a point not lost on management. University
students, academics and managers have a shared interest in
boosting the promotional capital of their university. Wernick
captures this culture well: it is 'a blend of consumerism and
managerial disciplinarity' (1991: 172).

To link Wernick's argument to Keat's analysis of practices,
I should like to take an example from the university in which
I work, the University of Nottingham. A few years ago a
student asked me if I could translate the Latin motto, *Sapientia
urbs conditur*; it means 'A city is built on wisdom'. Until the
1980s, this motto, which is part of the University's coat of
arms, was prominently displayed on University letterheads and
prospectuses. It was a fitting motto for its time of origin,
expressing the intellectual goals and civic pride of a provincial
university.

University College, Nottingham, was founded in 1881; like
similar foundations it was not permitted to confer its own
degrees, but instead awarded external degrees under licence
from the University of London. Heraldic arms were granted
in 1904 and confirmed in 1948, when the College received its
Royal Charter as the University of Nottingham. The official
heraldic description of the coat of arms reads as follows:
'Barry wavy of six argent and azure, a cross moline gules; on
a chief of the last an open book proper clasped or inscribed
with the words "Quaerenti Ostium" in Roman characters
sable between two domed towers also proper, that to the
dexter ensigned with an increscent of the first and that to the
sinister with an estoile also or.'

This is, in one perspective, medieval gibberish; but in many
cultures such condensed symbols, infused as they are with rich

historical allusions, are priceless. Money cannot buy them; all it can purchase is cheap fakes, the sort of history that is sold to gullible or ironic tourists. Yet since the 1980s the University of Nottingham crest has been rarely seen; it was displaced by a corporate logo purchased from a design consultancy. (The same is true of most British universities.) Letterheads, job advertisements and prospectuses all carry the logo; academics can even download it for use in their PowerPoint 'presentations', though not all do so. The logo is one aspect of the rebranding of the university as a modern corporation. It is a telling example of de-differentiation: the university is not just businesslike, it has become a business. In such a promotional culture, ironically, ancient universities that have spurned rebranding find their superiority confirmed. By rejecting the trappings of promotionalism they succeed in promoting themselves.

Even at the rebranded University of Nottingham, the heraldic crest is on display at what is for students and their families the supreme rite of passage: graduation. It was after graduation that I was asked to translate the motto; the student had seen it for the first time on his graduation certificate. Why not the logo? Given the logo's prominence this is not a frivolous question; why should a degree certificate not be graced with the proud logo? The answer, I believe, strikes at the heart of promotional culture and the reality of practices. The logo, and the corporate rhetoric and trappings that accompany it, are not addressed to students; *students are not the customer.* The customer is the state, which wants to know that public money is well spent and relies upon the apparatus of the quasi-market to be assured that it is so. This is not a free market, but a state-sponsored simulacrum of the market. To the state, universities are a business; to students, they are universities.

The case for the market rests heavily on the claim that markets make the consumer sovereign. The case of promotional culture in universities is merely one example to show that the claim is questionable.

The Market Experience

In *Martin Chuzzlewit* (1844), Charles Dickens describes the pleasure taken by Tom Pinch and his sister Ruth in

their regular walks through London's fruit and vegetable
market:

> Many and many a pleasant stroll they had in Covent Garden
> Market: snuffing up the perfume of the fruits and flowers,
> wondering at the magnificence of the pineapples and melons;
> catching glimpses down side avenues, of rows and rows of old
> women, seated on inverted baskets shelling peas; looking
> unutterable things at the fat bundles of asparagus with which
> the dainty shops were fortified as with a breastwork; and, at the
> herbalists' doors, gratefully inhaling scents as of veal-stuffing
> yet uncooked, dreamily mixed up with capsicums, brown-
> paper, seeds: even with hints of lusty snails and fine young curly
> leeches. Many and many a pleasant stroll they had among the
> poultry markets, where ducks and fowls, with necks unnatu-
> rally long, lay stretched out in pairs, ready for cooking; where
> there were speckled eggs in mossy baskets; white country
> sausages beyond impeachment by surviving cat or dog, or horse
> or donkey; new cheeses to any wild extent; live birds in coops
> and cages, looking much too big to be natural, in consequence
> of those receptacles being much too little; rabbits, alive and
> dead, innumerable. Many a pleasant stroll they had among the
> cool, refreshing, silvery fish-stalls, with a kind of moonlight
> effect about their stock in trade, excepting always for the ruddy
> lobsters. Many a pleasant stroll among the waggon-loads of
> fragrant hay, beneath which dogs and tired waggoners lay fast
> asleep, oblivious of the pieman and the public house.

As a boy, Dickens used to visit an uncle who lived in
Soho, close to Covent Garden. The future novelist took the
opportunity to visit the market whenever he could to soak
up its atmosphere. A child's fantasy of the market is recap-
tured in *Little Dorrit* (1857); her ideas are a swirl of imagin-
ative constructions of a market offering a profusion of
goods, a magical realm frequented by handsome gentlemen
and grand ladies, and far beyond the reach of her humble
relatives. Yet, based on her observations, Little Dorrit also
entertained

> desolate ideas of Covent Garden, as having all those arches in
> it, where the miserable children in rags among whom she had
> just now passed, like young rats, slunk and hid, fed on offal,
> huddled together for warmth, and were hunted about.

Dickens the social reformer is not sentimentally unaware of the significance of such human degradation, for he immediately adds: 'look to the rats young and old, all ye Barnacles, for before God they are eating away our foundations, and will bring the roofs on our heads!'

The stark reality of Covent Garden is also depicted in *Our Mutual Friend* (1865), where Dickens describes its sleazy allure:

> It may be the companionship of the nightly stir, or it may be the companionship of the gin and beer that slop about among carters and hucksters, or it may be the companionship of the trodden vegetable refuse which is so like their own dress that perhaps they take the Market for a great wardrobe; but be it what it may, you shall see no such individual drunkards on doorsteps anywhere, as there. Of dozing women-drunkards especially, you shall come upon such specimens there, in the morning sunlight, as you might seek out of doors in vain through London.

Must we choose between Dickens's rival descriptions of Covent Garden? The fact that we are dealing with a real market in a real time and place makes it easy to see the answer: that they are two sides of the same coin and therefore equally valid. Profusion and squalor, affluence and inequality, inclusion and exclusion, choice and dehumanization, freedom and exploitation: inescapable antinomies of the market experience.

When we turn to *the* market, an abstraction that floats free of any moorings in time and place, it becomes plausible to strike rigid postures for and against. Yet this, I would argue, is disastrous intellectually and politically. Co-ordination without a co-ordinator, co-ordination by mutual adjustment, is an element in all social settings. Even in a prison, social order is not simply a matter of coercion, and even in a community of saints, co-ordination is not achieved through value-consensus alone. A wealth of social theory recognizes this. Theorists as diverse as Anthony Giddens, Pierre Bourdieu and Harold Garfinkel, to take merely three outstanding examples, all emphasize the part played by practical consciousness and tacit knowledge, the 'feel for the game' without which social order would disintegrate. The same is true of Adam Smith, provided our view of him is not distorted by the lens of his neoliberal disciples.

In an essay written in the mid-1920s, John Maynard Keynes wrote: 'The political problem of mankind is to combine three things: economic efficiency, social justice, and individual liberty' (Keynes 1963/1931: 344). Free marketeers claim that the market achieves all three; their opponents deny that it achieves any of them. The wiser course may be to say that markets are a necessary but not sufficient condition of attaining the good society.

References

Akerlof, G. A. 1970: The market for 'lemons': qualitative uncertainty and the market mechanism. *Quarterly Journal of Economics*, 84, 488–500.

Aldridge, A. 1994: The construction of rational consumption in *Which?* magazine: the more blobs the better? *Sociology*, 28 (4), 899–912.

Aldridge, A. 1997: Engaging with promotional culture: organized consumerism and the personal financial services industry. *Sociology*, 31 (3), 389–408.

Aldridge, A. 1998: Reproducing the value of professional expertise in post-traditional culture: financial advice and the creation of the client. *Cultural Values*, 2 (4), 445–62.

Archer, M. S. and Tritter, J. Q. 2000: Introduction. In M. S. Archer and J. Q. Tritter (eds), *Rational Choice Theory: resisting colonization*. London and New York: Routledge, 1–16.

Backhouse, R. E. 2002: *The Penguin History of Economics*. London: Penguin.

Bauer, Y. 2002: *Rethinking the Holocaust*. New Haven: Yale University Press.

Bauman, Z. 1989: *Modernity and the Holocaust*. Cambridge: Polity.

Bauman, Z. 2000: *Liquid Modernity*. Cambridge: Polity.

Beck, U. 1992: *Risk Society: towards a new modernity*. London: Sage.

Beck, U. 2000: *What is Globalization?* Cambridge: Polity.

Becker, G. 1976: *The Economic Approach to Human Behavior*. Chicago: University of Chicago Press.

Beckford, J. A. 2000: When the battle's lost and won. In M. S. Archer and J. Q. Tritter (eds), *Rational Choice Theory: resisting colonization*. London and New York: Routledge, 219–33.

Bell, D. 1979: *The Cultural Contradictions of Capitalism*, 2nd edn. London: Heinemann.

Berlin, I. 1969: *Four Essays on Liberty*. Oxford: Oxford University Press.

Black, J. 1997: *A Dictionary of Economics*. Oxford: Oxford University Press.

Bork, R. H. 1993: *The Antitrust Paradox: a policy at war with itself*. New York: Free Press.

Bourdieu, P. 1984: *Distinction: a social critique of the judgement of taste*. London: Routledge.

Bourdieu, P. 1996: *The State Nobility: elite schools in the field of power*. Cambridge: Polity.

Bourdieu, P. 1998a: *Practical Reason: on the theory of action*. Cambridge: Polity.

Bourdieu, P. 1998b: *Acts of Resistance: against the new myths of our time*. Cambridge: Polity.

Bourdieu, P. 2000: *Pascalian Meditations*. Cambridge: Polity.

Braudel, F. 1992: *The Wheels of Commerce: civilization and capitalism, 15th–18th century, volume II*. Berkeley: University of California Press.

Cahill, D. 2004: New class discourse and the construction of left-wing elites. In M. Sawer and B. Hindess (eds), *Us and Them: anti-elitism in Australia*. Perth: API Network.

Callinicos, A. 2001: *Against the Third Way: an anti-capitalist critique*. Cambridge: Polity.

Callinicos, A. 2003: *An Anti-Capitalist Manifesto*. Cambridge: Polity.

Callon, M. 1998: The embeddedness of economic markets in economics. In M. Callon (ed.), *The Laws of the Markets*. Oxford: Blackwell, 1–57.

Carrier, J. G. 1997: Introduction. In J. G. Carrier (ed.), *Meanings of the Market: the free market in western culture*. Oxford and New York: Berg, 1–67.

Castells, M. 2000: *The Rise of the Network Society*. Oxford: Blackwell.

Davis, J. 1992: *Exchange*. Minneapolis: University of Minnesota Press.

Dingwall, R. 1999: Professions and social order in a global society. *International Review of Sociology*, 9(1), 131–40.

Dingwall, R. and Fenn, P. 1987: 'A respectable profession'? Sociological and economic perspectives on the regulation of professional services. *International Review of Law and Economics*, 7(1), 51–64.

Douglas, M. 1966: *Purity and Danger*. London: Routledge and Kegan Paul.

du Gay, P. and Pryke, M. (eds) 2002: *Cultural Economy: cultural analysis and commercial life*. London: Sage.

Durkheim, E. 1984/1897: *The Division of Labour in Society*. London: Routledge and Kegan Paul.

Fevre, R. 2003: *The New Sociology of Economic Behaviour*. London: Sage.

160 References

Fligstein, N. 2001: *The Architecture of Markets: an economic sociology of twenty-first century capitalist societies*. Princeton, NJ: Princeton University Press.

Frank, T. 2001: *One Market under God: extreme capitalism, market populism, and the end of economic democracy*. London: Secker and Warburg.

Freidson, E. 1975: *Profession of Medicine: a study of the sociology of applied knowledge*. New York: Dodd, Mead and Company.

Freidson, E. 2001: *Professionalism: the third logic*. Cambridge: Polity.

Friedman, M. 1953: *Essays in Positive Economics*. Chicago: University of Chicago Press.

Friedman, M. 1980: *Free to Choose: a personal statement*. London: Secker and Warburg.

Fukuyama, F. 1992: *The End of History and the Last Man*. Harmondsworth: Penguin.

Fukuyama, F. 1995: *Trust: the social virtues and the creation of prosperity*. London: Hamish Hamilton.

Galbraith, J. K. 1961: *The Great Crash 1929*. Harmondsworth, Penguin.

Galbraith, J. K. 2004: *The Economics of Innocent Fraud: truth for our time*. London: Allen Lane.

Gamble, A. 1996: *Hayek: the iron cage of liberty*. Cambridge: Polity.

Garfinkel, H. 1967: *Studies in Ethnomethodology*. Englewood Cliffs, NJ: Prentice-Hall.

Garfinkel, H. 2002: *Ethnomethodology's Program: working out Durkheim's aphorism*. Lanham, MD: Rowman and Littlefield.

Giddens, A. 1991: *Modernity and Self-Identity: self and society in the late modern age*. Cambridge: Polity.

Giddens, A. 1998: *The Third Way: the renewal of social democracy*. Cambridge: Polity.

Giddens, A. 2000: *The Third Way and its Critics*. Cambridge: Polity.

Goldthorpe, J. H. 1998: Rational action theory for sociology. *British Journal of Sociology*, 49 (2), 167–92.

Granovetter, M. 1985: Economic action and social structure: the problem of embeddedness. *American Journal of Sociology*, 91 (3), 481–510.

Gray, J. 1986: *Liberalism*. Milton Keynes: Open University Press.

Gregson, N. and Crewe, L. 2003: *Second-Hand Cultures*. Oxford: Berg.

Gudeman, S. 1986: *Economics as Culture: models and metaphors of livelihood*. London: Routledge.

Habermas, J. 1987: *The Theory of Communicative Action, vol. 2: Lifeworld and System: a critique of functionalist reason*. Cambridge: Polity.

Hall, S. 1988: Authoritarian populism: a reply to Jessop et al. In S. Hall, *The Hard Road to Renewal: Thatcherism and the crisis of the Left*, London and New York: Verso, 150–60.

Hamilton, B. 1986: *Religion in the Medieval West*. London: Arnold.

Hamilton, C. 2004: *Growth Fetish*. London: Pluto.

Hanlon, G. 1994: *The Commercialisation of Accountancy: flexible accumulation and the transformation of the service class*. London: Macmillan.

Hayek, F. A. 1994/1944: *The Road to Serfdom*. Chicago: University of Chicago Press.

Heelas, P. 1991: Reforming the self. In R. Keat and N. Abercrombie (eds), *Enterprise Culture*. London: Routledge, 72–90.

Held, D. 2004: *Global Covenant: the social democratic alternative to the Washington Consensus*. Cambridge: Polity.

Held, D., McGrew, A., Goldblatt, D. and Perraton, J. 1999: *Global Transformations: politics, economics and culture*. Cambridge: Polity.

Heritage, J. 1984. *Garfinkel and Ethnomethodology*. Cambridge: Polity.

Hirsch, P., Michaels, S. and Friedman, R. 1996: 'Dirty hands' versus 'clean models': is sociology in danger of being seduced by economics? In R. Swedberg (ed.), *Economic Sociology*, Cheltenham UK and Brookfield USA: Edward Elgar, 278–97.

Hirschman, A. O. 1970: *Exit, Voice, and Loyalty: responses to decline in firms, organizations, and states*. Cambridge, MA: Harvard University Press.

Hirschman, A. O. 1977: *The Passions and the Interests: political arguments for capitalism before its triumph*. Princeton, NJ: Princeton University Press.

Holton, R. J. 1992: *Economy and Society*. London and New York: Routledge.

Keat, R. 1991: Consumer sovereignty and the integrity of practices. In R. Keat and N. Abercrombie (eds), *Enterprise Culture*. London: Routledge, 216–30.

Keat, R. 1994: Scepticism, authority and the market. In R. Keat, N. Whiteley and N. Abercrombie (eds), *The Authority of the Consumer*. London and New York: Routledge, 23–42.

Keat, R. 2000: *Cultural Goods and the Limits of the Market*. London: Palgrave.

Keat, R. and Abercrombie, N. (eds) 1991: *Enterprise Culture*. London: Routledge.

Keynes, J. M. 1963/1931: *Essays in Persuasion*. New York, Norton.

Khurana, R. 2002: *Searching for a Corporate Savior: the irrational quest for charismatic CEOs*. Princeton, NJ: Princeton University Press.

Kuhn, T. 1962 *The Structure of Scientific Revolutions*. Chicago: Chicago University Press.

Lane, J. F. 2000: *Pierre Bourdieu: a critical introduction*. London and Sterling, VA: Pluto Press.

Lane, R. E. 1991: *The Market Experience*. Cambridge: Cambridge University Press.

Lavigne, M. 1999: *The Economics of Transition: from socialist economy to market economy*. Basingstoke: Palgrave.

Lebergott, S. 1993: *Pursuing Happiness: American consumers in the twentieth century*. Princeton, NJ: Princeton University Press.

Le Grand, J. 2003: *Motivation, Agency, and Public Policy: of knights and knaves, pawns and queens*. Oxford: Oxford University Press.

Liebowitz, S. J. and Margolis, S. E. 2001: *Winners, Losers and Microsoft: competition and antitrust in high technology*. Oakland, CA: Independent Institute.

Lindblom, C. E. 2002: *The Market System: what it is, how it works, and what to make of it*. New Haven and London: Yale University Press.

Lipsey, R. G. and Chrystal, K. A. 1999: *Principles of Economics, ninth edition*. Oxford: Oxford University Press.

Lukes, S. 1973: *Emile Durkheim: his life and work*. London: Allen Lane.

MacIntyre, A. 1981: *After Virtue*. London: Duckworth.

Malinowski, B. 1922: *Argonauts of the Western Pacific*. London: Routledge.

Marcuse, H. 1964: *One Dimensional Man: studies in the ideology of advanced industrial society*. London: Routledge and Kegan Paul.

Marx, K. and Engels, F. 2002/1848: *The Communist Manifesto*. London: Penguin.

Mauss, M. 1954/1925: *The Gift: forms and functions of exchange in archaic societies*. London: Cohen and West.

Miller, D. 1989: *Market, State, and Community: theoretical foundations of market socialism*. Oxford: Oxford University Press.

Muller, J. Z. 2003: *The Mind and the Market: capitalism in modern European thought*. New York: Random House.

O'Connell Davidson, J. 2003: 'Sleeping with the enemy'? Some problems with feminist abolitionist calls to penalise those who buy commercial sex. *Social Policy and Society*, 2 (1), 55–63.

Oldenburg, R. 1997: *The Great Good Place*. New York: Marlowe.

O'Neill, J. 1998: *The Market: ethics, knowledge and politics*. London and New York: Routledge.

Parry, J. and Bloch, M. 1989: Introduction: money and the morality of exchange. In J. Parry and M. Bloch (eds), *Money and the Morality of Exchange*, Cambridge: Cambridge University Press, 1–32.

Parsons, T. 1937: *The Structure of Social Action*. Glencoe, IL: Free Press.

Parsons, T. and Smelser, N. 1956: *Economy and Society: a study in the integration of economic and social theory*. Glencoe, IL: Free Press.

Philo, G. and Miller, D. 2001: Media/cultural studies and social science. In G. Philo and D. Miller (eds), *Market Killing: what the free market does and what social scientists can do about it*, London: Longman, 3–95.

Pierson, C. 1995: *Socialism after Communism: the new market socialism*. Cambridge: Polity.

Polanyi, K. 1957/1944: *The Great Transformation: the political and economic origins of our time*. Boston, MA: Beacon Press.

Pressberg, S. 1998: On financial frauds and their causes: investor over-confidence. *American Journal of Economics and Sociology*, 57 (4), 405–22.

Ray, L. and Sayer, A. (eds) 1999: *Culture and Economy: after the cultural turn*. London: Sage.

Riesman, D. 1961/1950: *The Lonely Crowd: a study of the changing American character*. New Haven: Yale University Press.

Ritzer, G. 1996: *The McDonaldization of Society: an investigation into the changing character of contemporary social life*. London: Sage.

Ritzer, G. 2004: *The Globalization of Nothing*. London: Sage.

Sahlins, M. 1972: *Stone Age Economics*. London: Tavistock.

Saunders, P. 1995: *Capitalism: a social audit*. Buckingham: Open University Press.

Scalmer, S. and Goot, M. 2004: Elites constructing elites: News Limited's newspapers, 1996–2002. In M. Sawer and B. Hindess (eds), *Us and Them: anti-elitism in Australia*. Perth: API Network.

Schumpeter, J. 1943: *Capitalism, Socialism and Democracy*. London: Allen and Unwin.

Sennett, R. 1998: *The Corrosion of Character: the personal consequences of work in the new capitalism*. New York: Norton.

Sikka, P. 2003: The role of offshore financial centres in globalization. *Accounting Forum*, 27 (4), 365–99.

Simmel, G. 1950/1908: Knowledge, truth, and falsehood in human relations. In K. H. Wolff (ed.), *The Sociology of Georg Simmel*. New York: Free Press, 307–16.

Simmel, G. 1990/1907: *The Philosophy of Money*. London: Routledge.

Slater, D. 2002: Capturing markets from the economists. In P. du Gay and M. Pryke (eds), *Cultural Economy: cultural analysis and commercial life*. London: Sage, 59–77.

Slater, D. and Tonkiss, F. 2001: *Market Society: markets and modern social theory*. Cambridge: Polity.

Smart, B. 2003: *Economy, Culture and Society*. Buckingham and Philadelphia: Open University Press.

Smith, A. 1976/1776: *An Inquiry into the Nature and Causes of the Wealth of Nations* (2 vols, edited by R. H. Campbell and A. S. Skinner). Oxford: Clarendon Press.

Smith, A. 1976/1759: *The Theory of Moral Sentiments* (edited by D. D. Raphael and A. L. Macfie). Oxford: Clarendon Press.

Sommerville, C. J. 1992: *The Secularization of Early Modern England: from religious culture to religious faith*. New York: Oxford University Press.

Spillman, L. 1999: Enriching exchange: cultural dimensions of markets. *American Journal of Economics and Sociology*, 99 (4), 1–25.

Stark, R. and Bainbridge, W. S. 1987: *A Theory of Religion*. New Brunswick: Rutgers University Press.

Stewart, I. 1997: *The Magical Maze: seeing the world through mathematical eyes*. London: Weidenfeld and Nicolson.

Stiglitz, J. 2002: *Globalization and Its Discontents*. London: Penguin.

Strangleman, T. 2004: *Work Identity at the End of the Line? Privatization and culture change in the UK rail industry*. Basingstoke: Palgrave Macmillan.

Sutherland, S. 1992: *Irrationality: the enemy within*. London: Constable.

Taggart, P. 2000: *Populism*. Buckingham: Open University Press.

Taylor, C. 2004: *Modern Social Imaginaries*. London: Duke University Press.

Tillman, R. 2002: *Global Pirates: fraud in the offshore insurance industry*. Boston, MA: Northeastern University Press.

Tillman, R. 2003: Abandoned consumers: deregulation and fraud in the California auto industry. *Social Policy and Society*, 2 (1), 45–53.

Tomlinson, J. 1999: *Globalization and Culture*. Cambridge: Polity.

Touraine, A. 2001: *Beyond Neoliberalism*. Cambridge: Polity.

Urry, J. 2000: *Sociology Beyond Societies: mobilities for the twenty-first century*. London and New York: Routledge.

Urry, J. 2003: *Global Complexity*. Cambridge: Polity.

Walzer, M. 1983: *Spheres of Justice: a defense of pluralism and equality*. New York: Basic Books.

Weber, M. 1948/1923: The Protestant sects and the spirit of capitalism. In H. H. Gerth and C. W. Mills (eds), *From Max Weber: essays in sociology*. London: Routledge and Kegan Paul, 302–22.

Weber, M. 1964/1922: *The Theory of Social and Economic Organization*. New York: Free Press.

Wernick, A. 1991: *Promotional Culture: advertising, ideology and symbolic expression*. London: Sage.

Wrong, D. H. 1961: The oversocialized conception of man in modern sociology. *American Sociological Review*, 26: 183–93.

Zelizer, V. A. 1997: *The Social Meaning of Money: pin money, paychecks, poor relief, and other currencies*. Princeton, NJ: Princeton University Press.

Zelizer, V. A. 2001: Human values and the market: the case of life insurance and death in 19th-century America. In M. Granovetter and R. Swedberg (eds), *The Sociology of Economic Life*. Boulder, CO: Westview Press, 146–62.

Zelizer, V. A. 2002: Enter culture. In M. F. Guillén, R. Collins, P. England and M. Meyer (eds), *The New Economic Sociology: developments in an emerging field*. New York: Russell Sage Foundation, 101–25.

Index